HERBERT PEPPARD
THE ETERNAL MAN

by janice dickson

introduction by herbert peppard's children

 **FriesenPress**

Suite 300 - 990 Fort St
Victoria, BC, Canada, V8V 3K2
www.friesenpress.com

Copyright © 2015 by Janice Dickson
First Edition — 2015

Cover Design by Joanna Iossifidis

ISBN
978-1-4602-6223-8 (Hardcover)
978-1-4602-6224-5 (Paperback)
978-1-4602-6225-2 (eBook)

1. Biography & Autobiography, Historical

Distributed to the trade by The Ingram Book Company

table of contents

dedication

For Herbert Peppard and his family

"There comes a time in a person's life when they are forced to make a momentous decision. It is a decision that will influence the trail they will travel down the rest of their life."

Herbert Peppard

To publish Herbert Peppard's biography, I held an online crowd funding campaign. The following categories represent those who made significant contributions toward the campaign.

Paratrooper Contributors

Ann McKim

Beth Johnston

Brian Cummings, *Herb's nephew*

Candle Larkin, *Herb's granddaughter*

Chantal Da Silva

Charles R. MacKinlay

Corliss Olson and Douglas Drake

Dan

Darrell Hewer

David and Matilda Armstrong

Donna Dickson

Douglas A. Lane

Ginger and Brian Lafave, *Herb's grand-daughter and grandson-in-law*

Jennifer Berghuis

Keith Tomasek

Kevin Brock

Matthew Bailey

Marilyn DesRochers

Malcolm Macleod

Mike Renaud

Nikki Boyle

Peter Grant

Peter Moore

Peter Rogers

Rob LeForte

Suzanne Saunders

William H. Cummings, *Herb's nephew*

The Bronze Star Contributors

Betty Cummings, *Herb's sister*

Bill Peppard, *Herb's brother*

Drew Dudley

George Tratt, *Herb's FSSF army buddy and lifelong friend*

Luc Palardy

The Silver Star Contributors

Belinda and Gordon Rogers, *Herb's niece and her husband*

Bill Stephens

Bon Cummings, *Herb's niece*

Lark and Carmen Hewer, *Herb's daughter and son-in-law*

Rosalee Peppard Lockyer and Allan Lockyer,
   Herb's daughter and son-in-law

Congressional Gold Medal Contributors

Herb Peppard Jr. and Deborah Chadwick
   Peppard, *Herb's son and daughter-in-law*

Robert Dickson

introduction

From Lark Hewer

Janice Dickson opens the door into the life of an amazing man.

Herbert George Peppard has lived a humble, yet exceptional life. His strength of character, including honour, integrity, and a personal motto to "never give up" has helped guide him through his life. At age 20, Herb left his hometown, his precious parents and eight siblings, and joined the army. Herb had many life changing experiences and gained lifelong friends while serving his country.

'Herbert Peppard: The Eternal Man' takes us into Herb's diverse reality serving as a commando soldier.

Even though Herb became a decorated war hero, having served with the elite First Special Service Force, his greatest battle was not fought in World War II Italy. Herb was 31 when his beautiful, young wife Greta was suddenly stricken with a life threatening illness. Side-by-side they fought together.

Herb Peppard has lived every day with an uplifting and positive demeanor. He found time to upgrade his education while working, and eventually earned his Bachelor of Education degree. He taught his trade, electrical construction, at a vocational school. Herb developed his keen interest in health and fitness, which led him to become a competitive bodybuilder. He has been referred to as the Father of Nova Scotia Bodybuilding.

Herbert George Peppard is my father. He has lived an admirable and exemplary life. I have always felt loved, cherished, and blessed to have him as my Daddy, and my hero. As an adult I've shared many special times with him and feel honoured to have our close relationship. I was very moved when he entrusted me with the precious love letters he wrote to his sweetheart, my Mom, during WWII. He knew I loved a project and he wanted me to put them into a scrapbook. Through that process, which resulted in a three-volume record of the decade in his life from 1936-1946, I learned much more than I had known about my Dad. I was once again enriched by him and by his life, and our bond grew even stronger.

I am so grateful for the summers we share at our family cottage by the ocean. When we're together we sing, go for walks, he writes and I edit his stories, and we reminisce about friends and family, especially Mom. She was the great woman behind the great man.

My mother, Greta, survived polio, worked hard at rehabilitation and tried every task herself first, rarely asking for help unless completely necessary. She took typing classes, driving lessons, and reconnected with her love of painting. She created original works of art for each of us three adult children—what a treasure. She always had a youthful joie-de-vivre and her sparkling blue eyes lit up every room she entered. We were not raised by a "handicapped" woman but by a beautiful, vivacious, creative, loving mother and a handsome but humble, gentle man who grounded us with happiness and love, my Dad, Herb Peppard.

Herbert George Peppard, son of Herbert Peppard, grandson of Herbert Peppard I, father of Herbert Peppard IV, and grandfather of Herbert Peppard V, *is* The Eternal Man. He represents goodness in its highest form as a son, brother, soldier, friend, husband, father, grandfather, and great-grandfather.

His legacy will stand the test of time.

From Herb Peppard Jr.

I had often thought about Dad's positive approach to life. I was sure it must have been grounded in his war experiences. I imagined him in the middle of any one of the many battlefield hells his unit faced. I imagined that he promised himself that if he survived he would never complain or make life difficult for anyone again.

I never heard Dad complain. I never heard him whine or feel sorry for himself. I never heard him raise his voice. I never heard him swear with a curse stronger than "Sugar Tit."

Dad saw the bright side of everything. I remember our camping trips in particular. We would be trying to put up the tent in a howling gale, rain pelting us, and he would be singing and saying how lucky we were. I haven't gone camping since.

From Rosalee Peppard Lockyer

In 2012 our Dad had a desire to take his children to the eternal city of Rome to experience the Sistine Chapel and the Trevi Fountain. For the first time since we were little kids, we all flew out of our active lives in Australia, Ottawa, and Nova Scotia to go on a family adventure to Italy together. We spent 12 days in the footsteps of the First Special Service Force.

In the mountains of central Italy, we were immersed in the humbling history of Dad's life as a soldier. There, I had an epiphany. My father was trained as, and for three years was, a lethal weapon of the First Special Service Force, but when WWII was over he came home to his beloved family, married his sweetheart Greta, our beautiful mother, and truly lived the life he fought for.

He is my father, mentor, hero, and friend. I am his eternally grateful daughter.

HERBERT PEPPARD'S WWII STATIONS & BATTLE INVOLVEMENT

Monte la Difensa	**December 3-6, 1943**
Monte la Remetanea	**December 6-9, 1943**
Hill 720	**December 25, 1943**
Radicosa	**January 4, 1944**
Monte Majo	**January 6, 1944**
Monte Vischiataro	**January 8, 1944**
Anzio Beachhead	**February 2 - May 10, 1944**
Monte Arrestino	**May 25, 1944**
Rocca Massimo	**May 27, 1944**
Herb was injured in Anzio	**May 29, 1944**

FOURTEENTH ANTI-AIRCRAFT BATTERY 1940

Truro	Nova Scotia
Halifax	Nova Scotia
Isle-Maligne	Quebec
Debert	Nova Scotia
Torbay	Newfoundland & Labrador

FIRST CANADIAN PARACHUTE BATTALION 1942

Ottawa	Ontario
Fort Benning	Georgia
Shilo	Manitoba
Return to Fort Benning	Georgia

FIRST SPECIAL SERVICE FORCE 1942 - 1944

Fort Harrison in Helena	Montana	Newport News	Virginia
Camp Bradford	Virginia	Casablanca	Morocco
Fort Ethan Allen	Vermont	Oran	North Africa
San Francisco	California	Naples	Italy
Adak Island	Aleutians	Monte la Difensa	Italy
Amchitka Island	Aleutians	Anzio Beachhead	Italy
Kiska Island	Aleutians	Naples	Italy
Return to San Francisco	California	Rome	Italy
Return to Fort Ethan Allen	Vermont	Marseille	France
		Naples	Italy

FIRST CANADIAN PARACHUTE BATTALION 1944 - 1945

Bulford	England
Glasgow	Scotland
Truro	Nova Scotia *(on leave)*
Niagara	Ontario

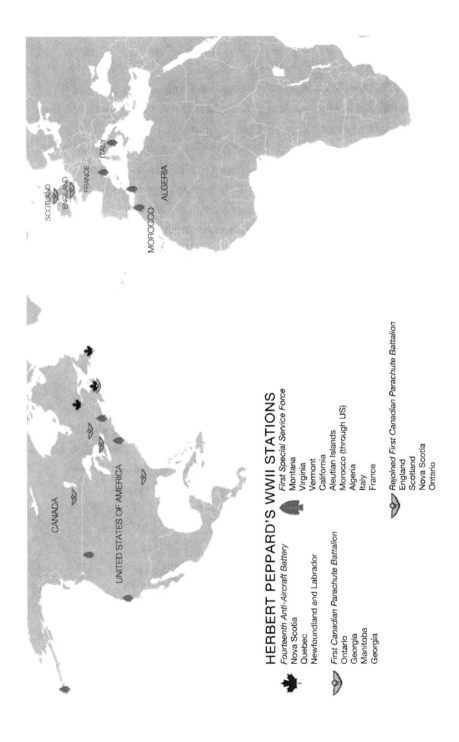

HERBERT PEPPARD'S WWII STATIONS

Fourteenth Anti-Aircraft Battery
Nova Scotia
Quebec
Newfoundland and Labrador

First Canadian Parachute Battalion
Ontario
Georgia
Manitoba
Georgia

First Special Service Force
Montana
Virginia
Vermont
California
Aleutian Islands
Morocco (through US)
Algeria
Italy
France

Rejoined First Canadian Parachute Battalion
England
Scotland
Nova Scotia
Ontario

December 19, 1943, Italy

Dear Mum,

What can I say now? For the second time I will go into action. I know from the last mission, war is <u>Hell</u>. I only hope I prove myself worthy of being a Canadian Soldier.

And Mum, what can I say to you? You're the one who stays behind and worries over me. Me, a son who was never worthy of such a mother. I've dreamed of coming home and getting married and settling down. And just between we two, I've had Greta MacPhee in mind. The Hell of it is; Would she accept? She may, and I base all my hopes on her saying "yes."

To Dad I say: I'm proud to be your son and you were always very dear to me even if we weren't the closest. I wish you would always plant poppies in your garden because I love them.

I also say good-bye (in case) to sister Dot, Iola, Louise, Pat, Ray, Albert, Betty and Billy and tell them Mum that I've always loved them dearly even though I have been a little lax in writing them. And also say a guy could never want a better bunch of brothers and sisters.

And now Mum back to you: I've planned lots of things for the time when I'd come home to you. I'd take you to shows, restaurants etc. I always was proud to walk down the street with you Mum, and hear the people whisper. "My! Isn't Mrs. Peppard young looking!" And so Mum I'll close with saying please don't grieve too much if I should be taken away because the worst thing I ever saw was the few times I witnessed you crying.

Good-Bye!

Chin-up!

Love,
Herbie

prologue

I open the screen door and let it rest on my back as I knock on Herbert Peppard's door and wait for him to let me in. I take a few deep breaths and look around the outside of his home. Flowers are just starting to poke through the soil on the right side of the step.

I had heard so much about the man I'm about to meet. I hear heavy footsteps come toward the door, followed by a booming voice.

"Come on in, come on in. Make yourself at home," he says to me as I walk in from the rain. He insists I keep my shoes on, regardless of how wet they are.

"They won't hurt anything," he assures me.

He leads me through a hallway full of black and white photos until we reach his kitchen. My gaze falls to the kitchen table. Photos from Herb's recent trip to India lay beneath a clear plastic tablecloth. He points out a photograph of himself on an elephant and another at the Taj Mahal.

As I sit across from Herb, fascinated by the photographs on his table and the body building photos hanging on the wall, I ask him, "has anyone ever asked you if they could write your biography?"

He shakes his head and smiles.

"Oh no, not yet, but I have written a book."

He disappears into his office and comes back with a book.

"The LightHearted Soldier," by Herbert Peppard.

I flip through his book, glancing quickly at the chapter titles—'The Reluctant Recruit,' 'Rest Easy Canada, I've joined the Army!' and observed that many included 'AWOL' in the title. He says it's mostly short stories from his war missions. He tells me to borrow it.

"I've got more material for you," he says, as he goes into his little office full of books and old photographs.

On his kitchen counter is a container of whey protein and beside it – a resistance band.

He emerges with a stack of neat purple folders. On the outside of each folder is a list that describes exactly what is in each. One folder, for example, contains all of the stories he wrote about events prior to the war; another contains only things that pertain to his life during the war. Another is about times after the war. I had no idea he had his life this organized.

"I also have a scrapbook that my daughter Lark made for me," Herb says, laying down a thick scrapbook labeled: WWII.

Flipping through the scrapbook, I find pictures of Herb and his army friends. But what really captivates my attention are the letters—messages to his parents and love letters sent to his wife Greta. Enthralled, I can't stop reading his love letters.

"Do you mind that I'm reading these?" I ask.

"Oh no, not at all," he says.

"I realize people these days may not be so romantic," he adds.

"May I use these letters throughout your biography?"

"Of course, of course," he assures me. Then he pulls out a small black diary.

"We weren't allowed to have a diary but I kept one anyway," he says, placing the tiny diary before me.

"Where did you hide it?" I ask.

"Oh, in a good place," he grins.

On the inside of the diary it says, "Memory is elusive, capture it." But there are few entries—he was too busy at that time to write, he says.

He offers me a cup of tea and apologizes for only having one cookie; he cuts it in two for us to share.

"So how long have you lived here?" I ask.

"I was born right here in this house," he says with a smile.

During my visit, I explain to Herb that I wish to write about his life, beginning with his childhood. I watch him look through his organized files; inside are stories that describe nearly every chapter of his life.

"My childhood? You want to begin with my childhood?" he says, rummaging through his files. "I seem to have lost my childhood," he laughs.

"I'm almost 93, my childhood was a little ways back," he grins.

His mother, Ida, and his father, Herb Sr., raised him in his house on Alice Street in Truro, Nova Scotia, along with his eight siblings: Dorothy, Iola, Louise (who were all older than Herb) and his five younger siblings: Patricia, Raymond, Albert, Betty, and Bill.

I ask him about growing up during the Depression and he says he didn't seem to notice; everyone was poor but they still played games like "kick the can." Herb's father was a locomotive fireman on the Canadian National Railway, but unfortunately there was not a lot of work.

"I love to write; I've written poetry, short stories about my family, and many stories have been published in the *Truro Daily News*," Herb says.

"Just one minute," he says to me, disappearing through the hall and into the TV room.

I sit at his kitchen table sipping on tea, captivated by the photos in his kitchen. There are photos of Herb and former Canadian prime minister Jean Chrétien; there is a photo of Herb and George W. Bush—and then there is a black and white photo on his fridge of a young man in an army uniform. I can't help but wonder who it is.

"I found some more stories," Herb says as he emerges from the TV room.

He started writing after the war - a passion that has stuck with him for his entire life.

"Here's one I wrote," Herb says, placing a short story in front of me.

It's entitled, "God's Gift to a Family—A Mother."

In this story, Herb describes his mother as courageous, loving, sacrificing, and determined.

"She was a mother of nine in the 1930s, and our father didn't have a regular income. She succeeded through her love and dedication," Herb says.

"Here's another one, about my father," Herb says, sliding another story across the table. This story is about an experience he had with his dad when he was seven years old. His dad gave his mom mayflowers for Mother's Day because he couldn't afford a gift.

"We laid in the grass and picked mayflowers. Lying there together, he talked to me as an equal," Herb says.

"How could I be equal to such a man?" he wrote in his story about his dad.

Herb's eyes met mine after we both looked at the photo on his fridge.

"That was my best friend, Smitty. He was killed in action...let me read you a poem," he says.

He pulls a poem from one of his files and belts the first line:

> We may forget how the ominous clouds
> Rolled o'er the sea from a distant shore.
> And called our young and precious men
> And plunged them into the hell of war.
> We may forget how the bulging ships
> Took from our land our pride and gems.
> We may forget all this - and yet,
> We will always remember them.
> We may forget those dark, dark days
> When all we knew was fear and death.
> When mighty armies met and clashed
> While the whole world waited - held its breath.
> We may forget how our young and brave
> Filled in the breach, the tide to stem.
> We may forget brave days of the past - but,
> We will always remember them.
> We may forget that glorious day
> When the gun-fire ceased, our boys came home.
> We may forget a mother's prayer
> As she knelt in the church to pray alone.
> We may forget how close we came
> To freedom's loss - through greed of men.
> We may forget all this – but, we vow,
> We will always remember them.

"I wrote that in 1984," says Herb.

"Why 1984?" I ask.

"I felt a pang of loneliness. I can't control when I'm reminded of friends I lost at war. It just happens sometimes, so I write."

one

"I wanted to be strong."

Herb Peppard

Herb shuffles his calendar card to the back of its box, revealing the new date: May 29th, 2012.

"There we go, now we have the right date. I like this kind of calendar much more than the kind that hangs on the wall," Herb tells me, admiring the purplish-blue irises on the calendar card.

Herb gets up from the kitchen table where we have met for our second interview. He pours two cups of tea. I notice his agenda.

"Do you mind?" I ask, curiously sliding his personal agenda in front of me.

"Not at all, but you probably won't find much in there," he says.

In his day-planner, Herb has documented everything he has done every single day. He lists his activities, whether it be going for a walk, meeting somebody for lunch, and with whom he's spoken on the phone.

"I have more if you're interested," he says, putting down the tea and milk on the table.

Herb disappears into his office and comes back with a stack of day-planners.

"I write everything," he tells me.

But his day-planners do not date all the way back to the summer of 1936 – and that's where we began.

"In the summer of 1936, I had to find a job," he starts.

At the time, no one could find work. On one hot day in June, he sat in his kitchen staring at his mother, Ida. She stared back. He was so strong and handsome then. I sit across from Herb in the very kitchen his mother told him to get a job, and imagine their conversation.

Most important, he was strong; and so it didn't take long for his mom to think of a job that would suit him.

"Why don't you go work for Uncle Lester?" asked Ida, referring to Herb's uncle who owned a farm. "Just wait, I'll get him on the telephone," she said before Herb even had a chance to answer.

She leaned against the kitchen cabinet and waited for Uncle Lester to pick up. Herb listened as his fate was sealed for the summer.

"Tomorrow?" Herb heard his mom ask.

"Tomorrow," Herb whispered to his mom.

She nodded. The next day, Herb started working on Lester's farm.

"I was paid in room and board and one bag of potatoes per day," Herb tells me. "After just two weeks of work, my parents' basement was overflowing with potatoes, the pile was this high!" Herb says, motioning with his arms.

Herb was helping with the fall harvest and he started to worry about showing up to school a month after classes had begun.

Now that Herb was 16 years old, he would attend the local high school, the 'Academy.' On his first day back, his mom helped him get ready.

"Ok Herbie, it's really time to get going—you're going to be late!" Ida Peppard called up the stairs. Her voice echoed through the narrow staircase, bouncing off the flowered wallpaper.

"I'm already a month late!" Herb called back.

He rummaged through his drawers trying to find something that didn't smell like potatoes. It didn't matter how late he was on that day, the teacher was unhappy with him for missing the start of school.

As students, they were expected to purchase their books. Like many families, Herb's couldn't afford to pay for his books. Herb said that one day while he was in class, his teacher, Miss MacLean asked him a history question.

"I'll never forget that day," Herb tells me.

"I can't answer that question; I don't have the book," Herb told his teacher. "Well what are you waiting for, Christmas?" she asked, causing the class to erupt in laughter at his expense.

The next day, he quit school. This time he found himself in their barn with his father.

"I have a friend at the lumberyard," his dad said.

Herb let out a deep sigh and put his head in his hands.

"Okay, I'll do it," he said.

The next day Herb woke early, put on his coveralls, a thick jacket and boots—all graciously donated by his father—and he left for the lumberyard. He thought it was strange to be walking in the opposite direction of school. But he didn't have far to go, the lumberyard was only five minutes away from his house. He would get used to it.

He walked into the lumberyard and looked for someone who might be in charge.

"Are you lost, son?" shouted a man as he continued to pile wood.

"I'm Herb Peppard, I'd like to work," he said.

"Head over to the barn and grab some gloves," the same man shouted again.

He made 15 cents an hour, or nine dollars a week. He worked 10 hours a day, six days a week. The conditions were rough, but he felt fortunate to have any kind of work. His job included piling lumber, supplied by nearby sawmills, to dry. Once dry, the lumber would be taken to the mill and planed. After it was dressed, it would be shipped out by railway boxcars to different customers.

Doug King, Freeman Wallace, and Herb, 17

To unwind after a long day of piling lumber, Herb went to Freeman Wallace's barn. They talked and played games there and it quickly became the place to hang out. One evening after work, Herb walked to the barn, but no one was there. He brushed woodchips from the old orange-plaid sofa and stretched out his legs. He tried to get comfortable but it seemed he had outgrown the length of the sofa. He stretched his legs over the far end and nuzzled his head into the arm. Within minutes he was asleep.

"Get up, get up!" Freeman yelled excitedly as he pushed his way through the barn doors.

Herb opened his eyes and shook his head. He had no idea how long he had been sleeping. But he did know that Freeman was excited about something.

"Win MacIntosh told me there's a guy at the other end of town who has a brand new barbell set! We have to go down and see it!" Freeman said.

"Wow! Well, let's go," Herb said. He had never seen a barbell set in his life, only in magazines. They walked to Duke Street and found the blacksmith's shop with the magnificent barbell set.

On the way, Herb thought about the first time he visited the blacksmith's shop. The shop intimidated him. It looked like a big open barn with no ceiling and had huge rafters going up to the peak. On one end, there was a smoking forge with a canopy to clear the smoke. The fire always seemed to be smoldering. Herb had heard that the fire was always left on. On one side, huge straps used to lift horses in the air hung down. That way, the blacksmith could shoe the horse without getting kicked.

Now, the building gave Herb a sense of wonder. It held a special place in Truro's history. Ed Ogilvie's father owned the shop and Ed owned the barbell. Ed was a few years older than Herb and Freeman, but he was always nice to them. When Herb saw the barbell, it was love at first sight.

"It's an Olympic Bar," Ed said.

Herb admired the weights. He put his hands on the shiny bar and it turned easily in his hands. "York" had been stamped on each large shiny black plate. York was short for "York Barbell Company." The company was located in York, Pennsylvania, and was owned by a World War I veteran, Bob Hoffman. Ed continued showing Herb and Freeman overhead lifts, known as Olympic Lifts. Herb and Freeman made a few awkward attempts at lifting the weights. Regardless of the challenge, Herb loved feeling his fingers wrapped around the cold, shiny bar. He struggled, but eventually surged the bar over his head. Feeling proud, he lowered the barbell to the wooden floor.

As the boys were getting ready to leave, Ed encouraged them to come back any time. Herb thanked him and said he'd be back. On their walk home, Herb and Freeman talked excitedly about testing their own strength. They couldn't stop thinking about the barbell.

"I suppose we're pretty good at lifting lumber, but never anything like today," Herb said.

"Remember that cement piece?" Freeman asked.

Herb nodded, knowing exactly what he was talking about. The boys never found out what its use was. It was shaped like a cone, and they called it Pothead, for no reason. It was close to the railway tracks and the boys would struggle with it until they got it close to their chests and then try to press it over their heads. Herb was the only one of the group that could push it up to arms length, but he opted not to remind Freeman of that.

"Freeman, do you think we could get big and strong if we lifted that barbell?" Herb asked.

"I don't know," Freeman said.

"People will think we are crazy lifting lumber all day and lifting weights at night," he said. But Herb had more on his mind.

He dreamed of being strong.

"I remember visiting the blacksmith's shop every day," Herb tells me.

He wanted to learn as much as he could about lifting. There were three lifts: the military press; the two-hand snatch; and the clean and jerk. The military press involved lifting the barbell up to your chest, standing at attention, with heels together and pushing it overhead without bending the knees. The two-hand snatch meant lifting the weight from the floor and snatching it overhead in one motion. Finally, the clean and jerk—the weight is clean to the chest and then jerked overhead. Soon, all the boys in town were joining Herb and Ed at the blacksmith's shop. It was a social place for Freeman, Doug, Pike, Don, Albert, Herb, and Ed—all the boys, all taking turns with the barbell.

One evening, a man named Mr. Jenkins stopped by the shop. He was older than the boys and taught at the Normal College. He looked to be about 35 to Herb. Herb couldn't help but notice the silver streak that ran from the front of his hair to the back. Mr. Jenkins wanted to start a weightlifting team in Truro. Ed and the boys were more than willing, and the Truro Weightlifting Club was formed.

Herb was envious of one of the members: Doug King. Doug was naturally strong and after a successful lift he would give a little laugh. The laugh was aggravating as he boasted of his lifting twice as much as the rest of the boys. Ed was also competitive and would challenge Doug to an arm wrestling contest. The two boys laid on the floor and locked hands. Herb watched Ed—it was always more entertaining to watch Doug's competition. There was a sparkle of determination in his eye. Herb saw this look many times and it meant one thing: *I'm going to be the one to beat Doug.*

They stretched out on the wood floor.

"Are you ready, Doug?" Ed asked confidently.

Doug shook his head and smiled. They clasped hands and Herb watched Ed's arm begin to tremble.

Doug took a deep breath and brought Ed's hand to the floor.

Then, he let out his little laugh.

It was a beautiful summer evening in July of 1938 and Herb had just celebrated his 18th birthday three days before. He decided he would spend some time with Freeman. Lately their conversations had been about—who he described as 'that goose-stepping madman in Berlin'—Adolf Hitler. The boys didn't take him seriously.

By now they had several official members of the clubhouse—also known as Freeman's barn: Bob MacKinnon, Doug King and his brother George, Freeman Wallace and his brother Suther, Win MacIntosh, and Herb. Bob was the eldest and loved to bully everyone who was smaller and weaker than him. Herb remembers getting in a fight with him and winning the fight—although, he still sports a yellow tooth because of it.

Herb and Freeman were much closer. They loved to play tricks on people.

That night they wanted to prank Bob. Bob smoked a pipe and always left his pipe and the can of tobacco, which he stole from his father, in the clubhouse.

"Let's sabotage Bob's tobacco can. We'll put some horse manure in the can and mix it with tobacco. When he starts inhaling these fumes, he'll curse and cough. He will be on the hunt for whoever pranked him. Then, we'll make our get-away," Herb said.

Freeman's eyes shone with excitement. First, they got the horse manure, which was easy because there was so much in the streets from the horse barns in the neighbourhood. Then, they mixed it with the tobacco in Bob's can. Anxious, the boys sat waiting for Bob to arrive. As Bob walked in, the boys tried their best not to smile. Bob went for his pipe and lit it up. The revolting smoke filled the clubhouse, but Bob continued smoking.

"Boy this tobacco is strong! Dad must have bought a new kind!" Bob yelled. The plan had backfired. Instead of watching Bob squirm in

8

discomfort, the boys sat with eyes watering and throats sore as they inhaled the disgusting smoke. Bob never mentioned the concoction.

Herb woke up the next morning with an awful taste in his mouth. He had tried to forget about the night before but he was reminded of it every time he swallowed. Herb washed, dressed, and left for Spencer Brothers and Turner lumberyard. He noticed more and more that every aspect of this thriving business was disappearing.

Herb looked at his reflection in the bathroom mirror. *You can do it, you are strong*, he told the mirror. He splashed water on his face and washed his hands. The smell of the soap his mom had in the bathroom always made him feel calm. It smelled like flowers. He closed his eyes, inhaled, and let out a deep breath.

He was both nervous and excited for his first weightlifting contest. Mr. Jenkins had set up the competition against the Halifax weightlifting team. Herb and three others piled into Mr. Jenkins's car, singing the whole way to Halifax. The team members included Mr. Jenkins, Doug, Ed, and Herb.

The men warmed up on stage before their lifts. The contest was in a large theatre. While they were warming up the seats were empty, and the thought of them being filled made Herb nervous. The 70-pound warm-up barbell was on stage for practice. After warming up, the team gathered backstage. Herb's heart pounded as the lights came on, blurring the faces and bodies of those in the audience. He stepped onto the stage and with all his strength, flung the weight. He threw the weight with such force that it slipped out of his hands and came crashing down over his head. Knocked to his knees by the blow, Herb fell, wounded more by the audience's laughter than the weight. Embarrassed, he left the stage.

Herb tried to compose himself and his team members encouraged him to keep lifting. In the end, he placed second in the competition. Doug finished first. He accomplished a new weightlifting record, which pleased the audience. Mr. Jenkins and Ed didn't do well, but they would all continue to practice and grow stronger. Herb wished more than anything for his feeling of embarrassment to leave him alone. He was lucky his friends didn't tease him too much.

It wasn't something a trip to the Brookfield Creamery for an ice cream couldn't fix. Every Sunday they went to the creamery; it was closed but they knew a few boys who worked there and they struck a deal. Herb, Freeman, and Doug would buy a gallon of ice cream for 99 cents. Of course, the Sunday creamery workers pocketed the cash, but they didn't care. The boys would eat ice cream and talk about the craziness that was going on in Europe. There was that man in Germany—always saluting. The boys talked about his goal – which was to make a "Super Race."

Being in their late teens, they didn't fully understand the severity, the horror of Hitler's ideologies and his plans, and they made fun of him.

They didn't know he would change the world forever.

But right now, that reality was not theirs—not yet.

Herb had no intentions of going to war. His job at the lumberyard bored him, but he would take boredom over fighting. Hitler had invaded Poland, but Herb continued the repetitive motion of piling lumber. He continued to lift weights and eat ice cream on Sundays.

He turned a blind eye to the stories in the *Halifax Herald*, but he couldn't help notice all of the officers in uniform in town. Hundreds of boys and men signed up. Canada wasn't ready for war. The number of men that enlisted outnumbered army supplies. Soldiers in town were without boots and even weapons.

Herb was sure that the sight of these soldiers made Truro residents nervous—especially the ones guarding the Salmon River Bridge.

They were dressed in civilian clothes and one carried a broom over his back.

He thought they looked ridiculous.

"Herb!"

Herb glanced up from his pile. He hadn't noticed how long he was staring into the wood. The motions were so repetitive.

He recognized the voice; it was Freeman calling. He snapped into reality. It had to be something...he sounded panicked.

"France has fallen," Freeman said, huffing and puffing and tripping as he came closer to Herb.

France had been demolished by the German blitzkrieg.

Next was the Battle of Britain. Was he missing out on something? Here he was, working for the Spencer Brothers and Turner lumberyard, piling wood and sitting quite comfortably.

"All of a sudden, I didn't feel comfortable staying in Truro," Herb tells me.

He was strong, intelligent, and healthy. There were few like him left in town.

That night when Herb walked home from the lumberyard, he wondered how many more times he would be making this walk.

"Have I given you enough information for today?" Herb asks.

I tell him I think it would be a good idea to call it a day and I help clear the table.

"I'm going to send you home with something," Herb says as he walks through the kitchen and into the living room.

"Here, take this, I marked my favourites," Herb says, handing me a little red book.

"Robert Service," is etched in faded gold into the book cover.

"His poems are my favourite," Herb says.

two

Herb worshipped war heroes of the past and he was proud of the Canadians who fought in the First World War. He read about the Battle of Vimy Ridge and recognized the soldiers who accomplished a victory many thought was impossible. These were Herb's heroes and he wanted to follow in their footsteps.

The day started off like any other. He walked to the lumberyard carrying the same thoughts as the night before.

Beside the lumberyard was the train station.

"Every day, I saw soldiers coming and going on the trains. That day it was particularly cold and rainy and I was loading and piling wood when a train full of soldiers came to a stop. Signs saying, 'Hitler, here we come!' lined the outside of the train," Herb tells me as we sip on tea at a small round table in his backyard. It is a cool June morning.

"I was outside, you see, piling lumber in the cold. I thought the soldiers looked warm and cozy inside their booths. I could even see some of the soldiers laughing at me through the train windows – they were yelling at me, 'sucker, sucker!'" he says.

Herb envied the soldiers for being warm and looking so comfortable in their uniforms. The next day, Herb and Freeman went to the Willow Street Armoury to enlist.

It was December 12, 1940, and he was young, strong, patriotic — and 20 years old. He saw war as an adventure — being wounded or killed were far from his mind.

The next day, Herb boarded the train and watched Truro disappear from his window. He would miss his family. He didn't know when he would be home, but he felt in his heart he was making the right decision. Not only was he patriotic and excited about adventures and travelling, but he also loved history and was excited to become a part of it.

The train was packed with young men and buzzed with anticipation. They travelled to Halifax where they would begin training.

Herb would spend the next eight months in Halifax with his unit, the Fourteenth Anti-Aircraft Battery, stationed at the Connolly Street Barracks.

Herb's role within his unit was to defend the city of Halifax through various drills, most of which meant standing guard.

"I spent a lot of time standing in the snow," he tells me.

While standing guard, he paced – but not far – and wiggled his toes in his boots, trying desperately to keep them warm. He counted snowflakes landing on his face. He thought snowflakes were beautiful. There were two weapons his unit trained with, and they were both three-inch anti-aircraft guns. On guard, Herb walked in circles in the snow. He was ready for a new assignment.

Herb was stationed in Halifax, then Québec to guard a power plant, then Debert, and finally Newfoundland, where he stayed for three months.

Then, he transferred out of the Fourteenth Anti-Aircraft Battery and on August 8th, 1942, Herb signed up to join the First Canadian Parachute Battalion. He was sent to Ottawa to join other volunteers before being sent to Fort Benning, Georgia, to train. It was in Georgia where Herb had his first jump. He thought about the training he had endured up until this point—running, hand-to-hand combat, chin-ups, pushups, and every physical test imaginable.

What would prepare him for this moment?

He sat in a plane with 29 other paratroop hopefuls. Herb took a look at his buddies. Their hands were shaking and as they helped adjust one another's gear, their hands slipped from sweat. Everybody was nervous. The jumpmaster barked at the men to get ready. They started checking and double-checking each other's gear until finally it was time to take the plunge.

Herb's first jump was from 1,200 feet. After two and a half seconds his parachute opened with a big jerk.

What a view, he thought, barreling toward the ground. He could see mountains for miles.

He hit the ground hard. They were instructed to tumble; a lot easier said than done. After five parachute jumps, Herb earned his wings and a pair of tall, shiny brown jump-boots. He felt so proud.

One afternoon, in late November, the unit was called to stand in front of a Canadian officer named Captain Becket. He said he was looking for volunteers for a new unit called the Second Canadian Parachute Battalion.

Ninety-seven of the 127 men who stood in front of Captain Becket that day volunteered. Herb was one of them.

The new unit boarded a train and left Georgia for Helena, Montana and to their new base; Fort William Henry Harrison.

When they arrived, things weren't what they expected. The Second Canadian Parachute Battalion didn't exist. The unit they *actually* signed up for was an elite group; the first of its kind. The best Canadians and Americans together in one force. It was so secret, in fact, they weren't even told the name in advance.

It was the First Special Service Force, FSSF for short.

Their first task was to get introduced to their new weapon — the Garand M1, a semi-automatic rifle. They trained by firing at close-range targets. As they improved, they moved the targets back. Herb trained beside Tommy Prince, another member of the FSSF. Tommy was skilled with his rifle and Herb copied his every move. When the targets were collected Herb tied Tommy for third. Tommy couldn't believe Herb tied him; he was bewildered and impressed because Herb had said he was inexperienced.

"He said—I thought you didn't know how to do this," Herb told me of Tommy Prince.

"He is Canada's most decorated Aboriginal veteran," Herb says.

The men were placed into companies within regiments of the FSSF. Herb was put in the first company, first regiment (1-1) on the 60-mm mortar crew. The other three members became his very best friends—Jim O'Brien, George Tratt, and George Smith, otherwise known as Smitty.

The boys were excited about their new unit. It seemed like every day they were learning more about this 'secret service force.' Their equipment was advanced—they wouldn't use artillery or tanks. They had light weapons so they could travel a great distance with everything on their backs.

They had tommy guns, a bazooka, M1 semi-automatic rifles, a light machine gun, and a 60-MM mortar.

They trained Monday through Saturday. Mornings often started as early as 4:30 a.m. Training was intense but they were going to be one of the best-trained army units in the world. Mountains surrounded the camp, so training included mountain climbing, parachuting, and also hand-to-hand combat and combat skills training, including skiing.

Herb felt the rough snow underneath him as he kept up with his buddies during an afternoon skiing drill. This was his first time skiing. Every once in a while there was a patch of ice, followed by little hard clumps of snow—so hard they were like rocks. He felt his skis slip from his control and before he had time to find his balance, he was on the ground. His right leg ached. *Oh no*, he thought— *I can't be injured already*. But he was, Herb had broken his right leg.

He was out of commission for six weeks—but his injury didn't slow him down after he recovered.

The First Special Service Force practicing parachute jumps.

On January 16th, 1943, Herb decided to leave Montana and go home to see his family. It was a spontaneous decision made along with 16 other soldiers after they received a big paycheck. It was their first pay in a month because of travel and joining the new unit. Herb earned $123.80. He thought he was rich.

It only took a moment for the boys to decide how they would spend their money. They were going home — home to Canada. Knowing that they would be denied the permission to leave, they decided to break the rules.

The soldiers fled while it was dark and jogged to the bus, laughing and whispering all the while. So far, the coast was clear. All 17 boarded the bus in Helena and they were headed straight for the Alberta border. They sang all night long. Herb couldn't believe their luck. He anticipated that they could be pulled over and arrested at any time.

Leaving an army camp without leave—going AWOL— is a serious offence.

When their bus stopped 50 miles short of the Canadian border, the celebrations quickly came to an end. The bus driver yelled for them to get off.

Herb looked around nervously as they were led into a bright office. Afterwards, they were ushered down a hallway and then, he noticed the cells.

All 17 escapees were put into the same jail cell. At first they grumbled and complained. Just an hour earlier they were singing and thinking about their homes. Now they shared a cold cell.

Before too long they were back to their happy ways, joking and playing cards.

To their surprise, the sheriff approached their cell with an offer almost too good to be true.

As it turns out, the town they were in, Shelby, Montana, rarely had visits from soldiers; so the mayor insisted they have a fun night in Shelby, on the house. The only condition was that they return to jail at the end of the evening.

Herb ate steak and onions, four big pieces of apple pie, and drank three coffees. He was denied the opportunity to go home, but good food was the next best thing. Herb and a few others—who opted not to go to the bar— went to the movies.

Entertained and fed, they returned to their cell feeling pretty good about themselves.

The reality of their stupidity sunk in the next morning when ten angry military police officers arrived to pick them up. The angry officers ordered them to file into an army truck.

The punishment was most severe for Herb; he lost his corporal stripes and some of his pay. None of the group's punishment seemed to be too harsh. Herb figured the army probably thought of them as dumb criminals with a poorly executed plan. It was just too stupid to be taken seriously.

Now, it was time to plan their next trip—and this time, it wasn't a breakaway road trip to Canada.

The FSSF went to Virginia for the spring of 1943 where they had amphibious training. Here they learned how to get from ship to shore in rubber boats. This was important because often ships couldn't get to shore, so navigating a rubber boat was the only way to travel.

A few days later, the FSSF took the train to Camp Bradford, Virginia, for amphibious landing training. In seven-man rubber boats, they worked together to direct the boat along the beach.

Three men straddled each side of the rubber boat—one leg in the water, the other in the boat. The seventh man steered.

Herb thought this particular training exercise was a lot of fun. At least it was fun that day. In their issued bathing suits they splashed around in their boats—challenging other boats head-on and throwing the other soldiers into the cool waters.

He liked the fact that everyone was equal in their bathing suits—no uniform meant little authority.

Maneuvering rubber boats was just the beginning of their amphibious landing training. The next drill was ship-to-shore attack.

These drills started on board ships about a mile from shore. The men frantically climbed down rope ladders, landing in a rubber boat or a smaller vessel. They sailed to shore and then stormed the beach, yelling like a pack of wild men.

After the force spent the spring in Virginia, they travelled by train to Fort Ethan Allen in Vermont for the summer.

From Vermont, the FSSF took the train to a base in San Francisco, where they waited to be sent on their first mission. They departed July 12 on the SS Nathaniel Wyeth.

When the ship sailed through San Francisco Bay, Herb watched in awe as they sailed under the Golden Gate Bridge. The water was calm and the bridge glistened in the sun. He cherished that moment, knowing it would be rough at sea.

The force's commanding officer, Colonel Robert T. Frederick, announced on the ship's loudspeaker that they were heading to the Aleutian Islands because he had heard Japanese soldiers were invading. It was rumoured Japanese soldiers were taking that particular route into North America. Taking back Kiska Island was the FSSF's first mission.

The day the ship left port, Herb told himself he would not be sick, but it wasn't long before his body succumbed to the rolling waves. Throwing up over the side of the boat meant being mindful of the direction of the wind, or else it would blow right back in his face.

The Japanese army also occupied Attu, a neighbouring island of Kiska.

They soon learned that the U.S. had taken over Attu and 31 of 2,300 Japanese soldiers were taken prisoner. Herb heard that the remaining 2,269 were killed.

With each wave Herb felt another bout of motion sickness. He spent most of his time in his bunk, waiting it out. He laid on his back and rubbed his stomach. He tried his best to keep his eyes open; as soon as they shut he felt a sweeping rush of nausea.

Their convoy picked up additional ships off Vancouver on their way to Kiska. Both Americans and Canadians made up their task force of 30,000 soldiers. They were told the Japanese army only had 11,000 soldiers.

The FSSF stopped at the island of Adak and then the island of Amchitka—both foggy, barren, and moss covered.

Amchitka became home for the time being and Herb couldn't have been happier to be on land. He walked to a wooded area where they were told to pitch tents and with each step he felt his whole body swaying. He thought he was going to be relieved of his motion sickness on land but it followed him to shore.

Feeling as though he was still rocking from side to side, he pitched a tent and buried his food. Not wanting to break into their rations yet, the boys— George Tratt, Smitty, Jim O'Brien, and Herb went fishing.

They made hooks out of pins and with a little bit of bait they caught what Herb thought of as monster fish. They boiled water in a helmet over a fire and threw their catch in.

Days were spent in fierce training and at night they read poetry to each other. There were many other units also set up on Amchitka so the place hummed with energy—one night they even went to a makeshift movie theatre in a large army tent.

The day finally arrived when it was time to move in on Kiska and the Japanese soldiers. They boarded a landing ship specifically designed to carry tanks.

Reaching Kiska required amphibious landing. In small groups, the men loaded into rubber boats and made their way to northern barren land. After another bumpy trip, Herb kissed the ground when they finally reached Kiska.

The force was given orders—to hike through the barren lands, test their equipment, and watch for the enemy.

So far, there were no Japanese soldiers in sight.

They carefully made their way through thick fog along the shoreline.

Still nothing.

They were ordered back to their tents to await further instruction.

Herb kept his friends entertained by reading Robert Service poems and his favourite by Edgar Allan Poe, "The Raven."

"Once upon a midnight dreary, while I pondered weak and weary/ Over many a quaint and curious volume of forgotten lore," he read.

His friends listened, hanging on to every word. The enchanting words entertained the soldiers every night.

"We're moving out—back to the boats," ordered Colonel Frederick.

Once aboard the ship they found out an important announcement had been made on the radio the day before: the Japanese soldiers had fled. On August 31, 1943 the force arrived back in San Francisco before boarding a train to return to Fort Ethan Allan, Vermont, for more training.

Shortly after arriving, a rumour circulated that they would soon be going overseas. Many soldiers started applying for leave to visit their families one last time. Herb was denied a pass, but he went anyway— AWOL. It was his most important AWOL to date.

He was strolling along Prince Street in his hometown of Truro. In his uniform, ice cream in hand without a care in the world and no thoughts about war, when he heard someone calling after him. He looked up and saw the most beautiful girl he had ever seen. She was rushing over to him from across the street.

Herb looked around—surely this beautiful woman couldn't be talking to him.

"My name is Greta, you're in the same unit as my brother, Mosher MacPhee. Have you seen him?" she asked.

He did know Mosher. They had trained together with the First Canadian Parachute Battalion in Georgia, but he didn't transfer to the FSSF with Herb.

Herb explained that Mosher would have been transferred to the FSSF but he broke his ankle shortly before the recruitment. After chatting for a few minutes, Herb managed to muster up the courage to ask her on a date and she said yes. They went to the Royal Theatre. Herb was lucky she said yes because she was supposed to go on a date with a member of the English Air Force named Walter. Greta convinced one of her girlfriends to go with him instead, so she could go with Herb.

They managed to see each other a second time for a walk through Victoria Park. They held hands and sang together. He was overwhelmed with happiness. But the reality was Herb would have to return to his unit and he was worried Greta would eventually forget about him. She gave him her photo and he vowed to carry it with him everywhere he went.

Herb decided that not even the threat of punishment from his commanding officer could bring him down from the clouds.

Although he had no regrets about going AWOL, Herb knew he would be in some trouble for leaving. He wrote a letter to Major Becket, to let him know he would be back soon.

One of Herb's buddies happened to be with Major Becket when he read the letter aloud and said, "who in the hell does he think he is?"

For Herb, it was well worth it to spend time with his parents and meet this beautiful woman, regardless of the punishment awaiting him.

When he returned to Fort Ethan Allan, he was anxious about seeing Major Becket.

"It seems to me, Peppard, that you soldier when you want to and take a leave whenever you want to," Major Becket said sternly.

Major Becket's face was bright red and he was breathing heavily. Herb tried not to look into his eyes.

Herb was sentenced to 28 days in army jail and docked a month's pay. First he was marched to his barracks where he collected his things. His buddies greeted him, anxious to know what the Major had to say. They were just as upset as Herb when he told them he was to spend 28 days in the guardhouse.

Two military police officers took Herb to his new home. They shoved him in the cell with his five new roommates. Now he really felt like a criminal.

In jail, Herb thought about their commanding officer, Colonel Frederick. He was in his thirties but often soldiers called him 'The Old Man.' Herb heard he was a force to be reckoned with.

He also thought about Major Becket. He was fully within his rights to punish him. He had committed a crime, again. He was a repeat AWOL offender. But it was never a premeditated act. He didn't plan his AWOL offences in advance. He wasn't hurting anybody. He just wanted a break. He wanted a break from orders, marching, and army routine.

Lying on the tough mattress, Herb thought about all of the times he went AWOL. That was the purpose of jail, after all, to think about everything you've done. In addition to going AWOL to Canada—the time they were caught, and home on vacation—there were two other times. One time he had leave to go to Montreal, but he returned three days late; and another time he had permission to go home and returned four days late.

"Wow—that's a lot of AWOLs," Herb said aloud, staring at the ceiling.

Herb served twenty-four days in jail; he was let out four days early for good behaviour.

But it was in jail where Herb started writing to Greta.

October 6, 1943, Vermont

Dearest Greta,

At last! A letter from you! Aren't you ashamed of yourself keeping me writing like that? What!! You're not! Wait until I get a hold of you.

I got a letter from Mum yesterday so I'm pretty well satisfied now for a while.

Mum sent all the pictures and Boy! They came out swell! You took a swell picture up by your house—you know the one of you, you mum, your cousin and me. But sad to say I look at another picture and there was the same group except for me and my chief rival for your affections was standing there pretty handsome as you please in my place. Was I ever jealous! By – the – way- you never mentioned him in your letter and I must tell you although I dislike him as a rival I still admire him as a good guy and a damn fine sport. Fortunately for me he lacks my selfish qualities. Now here's something I want you to do if you have the spunk to, (and I think you have) go up home to Mum and ask to see the pictures and the ones you want you can take the negatives of them and get them developed. Cheap-skate aren't I? The address is 17 Alice Street. (Pardon me for an hour I have to go out and do some foot-drill) (I got in from drill but I'm going to take a shave and shower. Want to join me? oh! what am I saying? hold it I'll be right with you) Well, here I am again fresh as a daisy now, as I was saying, go and see mum as I wrote to her yesterday that you were going to drop in on her so she'll be expecting you and she'll be dressed up every day for fear you'll pop in on her. So please go and see her because you wouldn't want poor mum to be dressed up all the time as you can imagine how uncomfortable it would be for her. Ask her to show you all the pictures she has in the house and if there's any in my collection you wish to keep you're welcome to them.

I'll give you a tip for when you go up home. Mum's like me she thinks everybody's "stuck up" and she may be a little distant at first (like me) but you just act natural and she'll be writing to me something like this: --"She's a lovely girl Herbie. How did you ever get to know a nice girl like that?" then I'll have to confess to her that you were just being nice to me because I knew your brother, Mosher. But please go up or I'll kick the hell out of you.

Mum wrote and said the M.P'S were up home looking for me after I'd gone. They went upstairs and they yelled down: "You'd better give him up" mum yelled back – "If you find him you can have him" (of course they didn't find him) I guess mum got a great kick out of that. We have an hours foot-drill every night after supper. It's not too bad but it gets monotonous.

I'd give you all the money in my possession 16 cents to have seen you open that butterfly card. I can just picture your expression and every time I think of it I have a big laugh all by myself. And about that change, you're the worst talking girl I've ever seen.

About that Chinese writing why don't you take it with you when you go to a Chinese restaurant and ask the chinaman what it means. I double dare you.

And again what's the low-down on all this travelling we're going to do? You seem to forget about that house. What are we going to do? Travel first or build the house first?

Where are you studying short-hand and typewriting, up above the bank?

I'm glad your apples are sweeter because they were the sourest damn apples I ever tasted!

I guess Mum got all the souvenirs that I got in Kiska. I got one of the fellows (who really had a fun laugh) to take them home with him to Halifax and mail them from there but they wouldn't let him mail them so I guess sister (Dot) lives with him in Halifax went and got them. So ask mum to show them to you. I'll send you a piece of jap writing-paper I got up in Kiska in this letter and I'll send a cake of Japanese soap to you later. Hope they'll let it go through.

Just got a letter from my sister Louise. You know the one we visited but she wasn't at home!! thief!

I'm sure glad that picture of me and your mum came out good. I told her a dirty joke to make her laugh but of course she wouldn't tell you that because you're too young.

And now to give you hell (which you deserved) What's the idea? You wrote me three nice big pages. (Although you could have written more), and not a word how much you love me. Or do you care for me at all?

All the time you were likely thinking: "He'll be going overseas soon so I'll be nice to him. And so you finished your letter with a beautiful- "bye now"

When all along I was praying you'd say "closing with a big kiss," and your lip-imprints were there in lip-stick.

Well, must close now as you see I haven't anything to write about.

Hello! To your Mum and the folks and all my love you

Love + Kisses Herbie

P.S,
All I have to write with is a pencil and no eraser so if I make a mistake it's too bad.

P.P.P.S, got the petals of a flower you sent. Thanks! a lot.

P.S may see Mosher soon.

My return address:
F.85014 Pte. Peppard, G.H
1st Day. 1st Reg
1st special service force
Fort Ethan Allen
Vermont, U.S.A

P.P.S
I'll write once a week whether I hear from you or not. Please do the same Greta.

Tuesday October 19, 1943 Vermont

Dearest Greta -

Just finished writing to your mum so here goes for you.

Got your letter O.K and its swell hearing from you. I nearly kill the mail man every day. Wondering, hoping, praying – I hope Greta wrote to me. And then I turn away tears running down my cheeks, no letter again. The boys try to cheer me up but they can't do a thing for me. You see what you're doing to me?

Glad you like my letters Greta and if I'd known your boss was watching you when you read them I'd have put more crazy stuff in them. I bet you were embarrassed.

I can't explain my being so foolish. Here's something you may not believe and I don't give a damn whether you do or not. I wake up some mornings happy as Hell. I'm too happy to get up and too happy to stay in bed. Perhaps I am just content. Perhaps I'm crazy. Am I? You don't have to answer that question.

I got out of jail Friday as I was a good boy. They gave me four days off for good behavior. So I only served twenty-four days. I'm glad I got out for one reason and that is because mum and that damn sister, Louise were always teasing me about being a jail-bird.

By the way if you happen to see Louise on the street if you recognize her, go and confess about breaking into her house and raiding her pantry. She got a Hell of a big kick out of that. She's a swell girl! Her baby Russell (jr) is real cute. Peppard in him I guess don't say that's not or I'll be angry.

So you and Walter had a swell time on the bike ride eh? I'm glad you're having a good time. I won't say that I'm jealous but I am! Of course you don't love him as much as you like love me. What! You don't love me? Well, you'll learn, and if absence makes the heart grow fonder I'll stay away for three years, then will I ever get a swell welcome when I come back to you.

Truthfully Greta, I think this war will last for five more years. However, when we beat Hitler they may give us leave home before we tackle Japan. Something to look forward to though.

The boys were pretty happy to see me back in the Company—they like me because I'm so damn crazy I guess. They were telling me they went on a route march a few nights before I got out of jail. They said they were planning on raiding the guard-house and taking me with them. They miss my singing on the marches. I can't sing worth a damn but I can really make myself heard. I'm glad they didn't get me as the march was thirty-two miles and I'm such a lazy devil.

I have no marker for this writing paper so excuse it if I gotten get writing uphill.

Mum said you didn't get up to see her. She said you must be awful shy. I told her you were, and I should know.

So you bought a $50 War Bond. Good for you! I signed for one when I was in Norfolk, Virginia. They take $8.60 off a month for six months. I'll have it paid for the last of this month. I signed it over to Mum.

I never told you of my travels did I Greta? If you wish to hear of them just say so and I'll tell you all about them. I didn't want to talk when I was with you anyway.

What's the "E" stand for in your name? Eve, Ethel, Evangeline, Esther? Tell me Greta, Please.

Now what's this "kiss for good-luck" all about? Do you mean to say you were just being nice to me when I was home and that you didn't care a damn for me. Did you think: --"He has a slight chance of being killed so I'll make this leave happy for him and let him have a few kisses. Gee! He's a persistent devil!" Do you realize my chances of being killed are 1000 to 1. I'm such a lucky devil.

You were talking about the moon Greta! I'll bet it was pretty that night but why shouldn't it be in the prettiest town in the world? No argument there I guess.

We had a physical endurance test Saturday. The first excer exercise was push-ups. I did forty-nine and it was the most in our Company. Was I ever happy. (But I feel weak beside Mosher he can do fifty with one hand.)

Must close now.

Love to Walter (What am I saying?)

All my Love and lots of kisses,

Yours,
Herbie.

F.85014 Pte. Peppard. G.H.
1ST. Coy. 1st Reg.
1ST Special Service Force
Fort Ethan Allen Vt. U.S.A

On October 28, 1943, the FSSF shipped out of Newport News, Virginia, and set out to cross the Atlantic on the Empress of Scotland. The ship was an ocean liner—meant for long journeys—and although comfortable, it wasn't a military vessel. It took six days to sail to Casablanca, Morocco.

The force climbed a hill that overlooked the city and started pitching their tents. Herb stood at the top of the hill and looked at the white houses that shone in the sunlight. It was beautiful. Herb was proud to be a part of this special force. They wore red shoulder patches on the sleeve of their uniforms. The patch was in the shape of a spearhead and showed the letters USA, CANADA.

Despite being from two countries, they were united as one. Herb sat on a soft grassy patch on the edge of the hill. He pulled out small letter paper that said 'V-mail' and wrote Greta and his mother letters.

Dearest Mum,

Well Mum, we crossed the Atlantic O.K and it was a swell trip. I'd like to tell you all about it and also about the country here and how the people live but that's impossible as you realize. But I promise to get some souvenirs and bring them back home with me.

We sleep in tents here, six of us to a tent. Of course Smith is with me. We have a swell time.

We have four flags flying outside our tent. Tratt (friend of mine) owns a Canadian and American one, and I own an English and Canadian flag. They really look good.

I'm going to try to send home ten more dollars a month. I don't know if they'll let me but I'll soon find out.

Love and kisses,

Herbie.

Dearest Greta,

Arrived safely. Just filled one of these out to Mum. Am feeling swell. Will write as soon as possible. Will write once a week to you even though I may not hear from you in quite some time. I still treasure that picture I have of you. (You know the one taken, the one you didn't like).

Love Herbie

Herb couldn't enjoy the view for long. They were ordered to pack up. The tents came down and they were brought to the railroad once again.

He looked at the train they were about to board. A sign read "Eight horses or 40 men." It was a boxcar train, used to move cattle.

They boarded the train and headed east across North Africa. It was uncomfortable. Every so often the train stopped so the men could relieve themselves. Sometimes it would be in the middle of a small town. Other times there was nothing around at all. They continued like this for three days.

The train stopped at Port Oran on the Mediterranean coast. Herb and his friends were so relieved to stretch their legs—and they didn't mind their first order, which was a route march around the community.

Herb took in his surroundings. No more white houses glistening in the sun. It was lush and beautiful. There were acres of olive trees, stretching as far as he could see.

The olives weren't ripe enough to eat—but the soldiers plucked them anyway and threw them at each other.

three

"I only hope I show myself worthy
of being a Canadian Soldier."

Herb Peppard

Staring into the rolling waves of the Northumberland Strait, Herb tells me from his cottage porch about the time he and the force sailed from Africa to Italy. The force boarded the USS Thomas Jefferson military vessel on November 12th and departed November 14th from Oran, North Africa. They sailed to Naples, Italy, now an Allied headquarters and staging area, and arrived on November 17th, 1943.

"Boy was I glad that trip was only a few days at sea because I was always getting so seasick," Herb says as he sips on lemonade. Herb and his daughter Lark were spending two weeks at his place in Brule.

"I think we've had this place since...1950 or around that time," Herb tells me, explaining that it had been in the family. As Herb tells me all about his stories in Italy, Lark shows me a scrapbook she made of their recent family trip to Italy and the mountains they visited where Herb's unit had fought.

"Once in Naples, Dad's unit prepared to join the Italian campaign," Lark says, pointing to Naples on a map.

"Yes and I was with some of my closest friends: Norm Gray, Jim O'Brien, and George Tratt when we pulled into the harbour," Herb adds.

"An Italian man took our photo shortly after we arrived," he says.

Norm Gray, Jim O'Brien, George Tratt, and Herb

As he stood with his buddies, he felt something in the pit of his stomach. It seemed like yesterday he was piling wood and now he was in Italy.

His unit was sent just outside of Naples to prepare to go. They had to get ready to be sent to the Front.

Herb stared in awe of Mount Vesuvius, but he and his unit had gotten their orders. They were being sent to the front lines and he had to leave the peace and safety of Naples behind.

They set up camp in a stone house in Santa Maria, a small town four hours north of Naples. German soldiers had been in the house at one point—they went to the trouble of destroying the rooms. It was better than tents or foxholes, Herb thought.

After setting up, they hiked through the mountains and tested their weapons. Herb was in the mortar crew and the caliber of their mortar was 60mm.

While Herb worked with this mortar crew, others were learning about the latest weapon: the bazooka.

It took two men to operate the bazooka, and there was a trigger and battery on its side. One person would load the gun and hook up the wires while the other waited for his signal to fire. Herb was just over 100 yards away from the bazooka crew when suddenly he heard a massive explosion. There was a thump on the ground and Herb saw a jagged piece of metal. He picked it up and realized it was a small piece of a helmet. Inside there was a part of a human skull with a few threads of hair on it. He shuddered, dropping the piece of helmet. A soldier from his outfit who had been laughing only minutes before.

Another close friend of Herb's, George Wright, told him that his officer ordered his crew to fire the bazooka. The gun was loaded, wires hooked and ready, and when they pulled the trigger nothing happened. George ordered the men to lay down the weapon and step away. He wanted experts to examine it in the event of a misfire. But his officer ordered him to tell the crew to fire the weapon. He refused. He didn't think it was safe.

The officer was mad at George and ordered two men from a different platoon to fire the bazooka. And they did. The gun exploded in their hands. One of the soldiers died instantly. The other was badly injured.

The young man cried, "My bum is cold!"

"You will be going home soon, son. You will be going home soon, son," said the Major.

"Will I see my mother? Will I see my mother?" he cried.

Then the boy was gone.

Major Becket told this story to the men later on. He kept saying, "he was just a boy."

November 16, 1943

My Dearest Greta,

Well Greta, I just finished writing to my first sweetheart, (Mum), and now it's your turn. Feel slighted? I hope so.

I sure hope you've been getting my letters of late although I must admit they're little more than notes.

We had good news the other day. They were going to lift the censorship a little and what a long letter I had planned! They were going to let us write about the place we're in, the natives, and also going to allow us to send souvenir money home. Needless to say they clamped down on censorship again and those privileges were taken away from us. Does that excuse this short letter? It doesn't? The Hell with it then I'm not going to try to make up any more excuses.

I must say they're (I must watch my English while I'm about it) there are a lot of things I miss about Truro. One of my special things was the Outports Hour over C.F.C.Y. I really liked that. Of course I don't get as much kick out of a radio-program as your Dad but I nevertheless enjoy some of them.

By-the-way Greta when is your birthday? Don't get me wrong now I don't intend to get you a present I just thought you'd ask me the same question and in a round-about way I'd be the one to get the present. Clever aren't I? Joking aside when is your birthday?

I must tell you about my friend little Smithy. I went into the wash-room last night and there he was looking in the mirror smiling to beat Hell at himself. He had a book in his hand so I snatched it away from him. The title of the book was: "How to win Friends and Influence People." That explained his strange behavior but I got a great laugh out of it. Now I can insult him or say anything I please and he'll agree with me.

You spoke of Walter in reference to Thanksgiving but you didn't say how he got along with his parachute-jumps. Did he go to Montreal after all or did the big shots change their minds at the last minute?

I have some souvenir money and will send you some as soon as possible. I saw our ideal house the other day. All it lacked was the stone walk. Of course we could easily fix that. I can just picture you carrying those big rocks from

*about half a mile away and me showing you how to arrange them. Ho! Hum!
Makes me tired to think of it.*

*Must close now. Say Hello! to your family and especially Mum MacPhee
and tell her I'll drop her a line next letter.*

*Am sending you something I cut out of a "Believe It or Not" book. Hope
you like it.*

All my love + kisses,
Herbie

F.85014 Pte. Peppard G.H.
1st Coy. 1ST Reg. 1st Spec. Serv. Force
A.P.O #4994
New York, N.Y

November 25, 1943, Italy

My Dearest Greta,

*Still no letter from you darling, how can I go on like this my heart is
broken? I know you don't believe this bull, but it's fun saying it. Truthfully
though Greta I haven't heard from Mum or you since I came over. I hope
you're getting my mail O.K. Now if I had a letter from you I'd know what you
were thinking and doing and then I could write a swell letter.*

*Of course I <u>can</u> tell you what Mum said in her last letter and that was
<u>long, long,</u> ago. Want to hear it? You don't? O.K here goes. She said my
grand-mother's in the family-way. Grandma's 105 years old so I have my
doubts. What do you think Greta? What? You're not going to speak to me
again? Is that any way to use such a nice boy as me? If you think that was
bad give me Hell, if you don't think it was bad I'll give you Hell.*

*Well, Greta, I'm getting along pretty well these days. We have a lot of
route-marches and the other day we climbed to top of a mountain. We ate
our dinner up there. (Canned rations of course). While eating we enjoyed*

the scenery and it was beautiful! Naturally it can't compare with Truro from Wood Street, but that's to be understood.

I got a letter from my sister Pat the other day and she's thinking of joining the C.W.A.C's. Dad+Mum's against it but Pat's stubborn as the devil. I gave her my consent so I imagine she'll go ahead and perhaps by now she's in the army.

It was American Thanksgiving Day today and we had Turkey! What a surprise!

You should see me now. Sitting writing to you by candle-light. It's true and it also helps build up an excuse for this bad writing.

I'll bet you had some swell apples this year. My mouth waters whenever I think of them. We used to go stealing apples up at MacKay's on Wood Street, also at John Kennedy's on Lyman Street. And many other places. Damn little thieves I imagine they called us the worst boys they ever saw!

Have you seen any movies lately? Or would you rather go down to Smith's Avenue and admire the houses? You would? O.K. put on a pair of low shoes and let's go.

I suppose it will be close to Xmas when you get this letter. I can see you eating Xmas dinner now. You have a nice contented smile on your face. God I'm jealous! I'm sorry I can't send you a present but I can wish you a <u>Very</u> Merry Xmas and a Happy New Year, and I also want to send you all my love.

Yours,
Herbie

Merry Xmas to all the MacPhee family.

F.85014 Pte. Peppard G.H.
1st Coy. 1ST Reg. 1st Spec. Serv. Force
A.P.O #4994
Postmaster New York, N.Y

Herb understood that they were in Italy to fight the enemy — the Nazis. He couldn't figure out where they were. He hadn't seen any and so far war wasn't what he expected.

The harsh truth revealed itself after he heard the moans of his wounded comrades. The German soldiers were using big guns that enabled them to kill people from over a mile away. They were tucked into all of the mountaintops shooting their victims from afar.

They were in Italy for two weeks before they saw action on the night of December 3rd. The battle on the Monte la Difensa was the force's baptism of fire.

Herb had been in battle for less than 24 hours when the realities of war shattered his ideas and dreams of life as a soldier. His unit's first objective was to take over this mountain held by the German soldiers. In single file, Herb and his unit climbed the 3,500-foot mountain in the cold, driving rain.

Monte la Difensa is grassy on one side with rough terrain on the other—knowing that the German soldiers expected their enemy to climb the grass side, the FSSF divided their ranks and sent the Second Regiment up the rough terrain and rock face cliff. They knew it was the only way to get up the mountain alive and to surprise the enemy.

Herb was with the First Company, First Regiment. They were halfway to the top when they came under heavy artillery and mortar fire. Herb was terrified. That day, they suffered many, many casualties.

Herb could hear his comrades moaning and crying. These were the ones who had been blown down the mountainside. With each ear-shattering explosion, Herb watched as men flew into the air.

They kept climbing, trudging up the only path, each clinging to the person in front of them as they scaled the mountain. They carried many weapons: tommy guns, rifles, machine guns, mortar guns, and bazookas.

With each cry Herb wondered when it would end, this hell.

He heard cries of, "Jesus," and of, "Mama."

They were quickly losing men so they were given a new order. Instead of moving forward, they would dig foxholes and stay put.

The next order came with great relief; to pull back and head down the mountain on the same path.

When they finally reached the bottom, Herb was exhausted but his nerves wouldn't allow him to fall asleep. He credited his resilience to training. Everybody remained focused and obeyed orders like they were taught and trained to do.

The next morning, Herb volunteered to return to the mountain to bring back the dead and wounded. It was a job few were willing to undertake, but Herb was strong and felt it was his duty. The volunteers were given Red Cross armbands to wear, which showed the enemy that they were on a mission of mercy and not to fire. They weren't allowed to carry weapons because they were on a peace mission to help the wounded and carry back the deceased. Despite his fears, the Germans soldiers didn't shoot while they wore Red Cross cloths on their arms.

With two other men, Herb carried a stretcher and had a pack made of wood on his back. He will never forget the first victim — a haunting headless corpse with both of his legs and arms missing. Herb and the others discussed what was to be done with the torso. Their job had been to carry down the dead and wounded and this man was completely unrecognizable.

They decided he deserved a proper burial, strapped him to the back of a pack board, and took turns carrying him down. Herb rested at the bottom of the mountain, praying for God to remove the horrific image of the casualty. The men rested for a while before returning up the mountain to retrieve the rest.

December 19, 1943, Italy

Dear Mum,

What can I say now? For the second time I go into action again. It won't be fun because I know from the last mission war is <u>Hell</u>. I only hope I show myself worthy of being a Canadian Soldier.

And Mum, what can I say to you? You're the one who stays behind and worries over me. Me, a son who was never worthy of such a mother. I've dreamed constantly of late of coming home and getting married just to settle down. And just between we two, Greta MacPhee has been the girl I've had in mind. The Hell of it is; Would she accept? She may, and I base all my hopes on her saying "yes."

To Dad I say: I'm proud to be your son and you were always very dear to me even if we weren't the closest. I wish you would always plant poppies in your garden because I love them.

I also say good-bye (in case) to sister Dot, Iola, Louise, Pat, Ray, Albert, Betty and Billy and tell them Mum that I've always loved them dearly even though I have been a little lax in writing them. And also say a guy could never want a better bunch of brothers and sisters.

And now Mum back to you: I've planned lots of things for the time when I'd come home to you. I'd take you to shows, restaurants etc. I always was proud to walk down the street with you Mum, and hear the people whisper. "My! Isn't Mrs. Peppard young looking!" And so Mum I'll close with saying please don't grieve too much if I should be taken away because the worst thing I ever saw was the few times I witnessed you crying.

Good-Bye!

<u>Chin-up!</u>

Love,
<u>Herbie</u>

It was Christmas Eve, 1943, and the force was ordered to take position on a mountain known as Hill 720. Cold rain belted Herb's face and he dreamt of his warm house on Alice Street in Truro. He would give anything to be there.

Despite being under heavy mortar fire, the men followed orders and proceeded to climb the mountain. It was a stormy night and shells were exploding everywhere.

They were led by Colonel Frederick who believed it was his duty to lead the force. He was wounded multiple times while leading the FSSF into action.

Finally, they reached the top of Hill 720. The German soldiers fled down the opposite side and the force dug themselves foxholes for the night.

Despite the darkness, and the toughness of the ground, Herb dug himself a little hole where he would rest. He was exhausted but he couldn't sleep because of the explosions.

Then he heard someone call out, "Pep," a nickname for Peppard.

Searching the area, Herb could see only foxholes. But in the foxhole next to him, just 30 feet away was 'Tiny Beacon'. Herb couldn't help but crack a smile at his friend from British Columbia.

Tiny asked Herb if he had any food.

He searched in his pack for any K-rations— his individual package of emergency foods. Yes he had a couple cans of spam. Tiny had a couple cans of cheese and so they traded, tossing their canned goods at each other.

Herb opened the can of cheese. *Pretty good*, he thought. He used his dry crackers to scoop out the cheese, washing it down with stale water.

He could only imagine the smell of his home in Truro this time of year — a warm turkey roasting in the oven and all the other fixings on the stove in harmony. Thinking about it was mouth-watering.

His canned cheese and crackers would have to do for now. He was soaked and inside a wet, muddy foxhole, but he was determined to enjoy his meal.

Then he heard Tiny yell, "Pep" again. "Pep."

Herb peeped over the edge of his foxhole and saw Tiny's big helmet and dirty face. His friend smiled through the mud and he had to shout over the explosions.

"Merry Christmas, Pep!" Tiny yelled.

As the night grew into day, the reality of casualties began to sink in. Herb learned that his best friend George Smith, otherwise known as Smitty, was killed.

A mortar shell exploded at his feet and he died instantly.

Smitty was in the same area as Herb when he was killed.

The FSSF resorted to a temporary makeshift area and Herb was promoted to Staff Sergeant. He knew he was likely taking the place of someone who was just killed.

"Smitty told us men something when we were overseas and I'll never forget it," Herb says as we sit inside the small waterfront cottage, taking in the warm August breeze.

"He received a letter from a girl he had been going with and she was pregnant. He asked us what to do."

Herb says he remembers all of the men encouraging him to marry her when he returned from the war.

"He said – 'that's what I'll do!'" Herb recalls Smitty wanting to marry the girl, and he was excited about the baby.

"Of course, he never returned."

four

"There are no atheists in foxholes."

Unknown

January 1, 1944

Hello sweetheart,

Well, Mum I'm happy to say I got two letters from you the other day. One was dated Nov 25th, the other was airmail, which you wrote Dec 2nd.

I'll write this "V" mail letter for now and when I get more time I'll write a longer letter.

I'm feeling very good but sorry to say I spent Xmas in a foxhole. No matter if I couldn't be home for Xmas I don't care where I spend it. Yes. I came out of action again and I'm not much the worse for wear and tear. Glad to hear Pat looks good in her uniform. I'd like to see her. I'm looking forward to Xmas parcel with mouth watering.

P.S. Please don't ask about Smith any more.

Love and Kisses to you and Peppard family.
Your loving son, Herbie.

January 1, 1944: Italy

Dearest Greta,

I'm in a pup-tent writing this so please excuse. They call them pup-tents because they're about big enough for a small dog but they squeeze two big men into one. The light I'm using and cramped quarters are my only excuses for this scribbling.

Here it is New Year's Day! We had turkey for dinner and it must have been a hard job to get it to us. I got a leg and part of the rear end but we won't talk about that. We were in action again Christmas and I spent Xmas Day in a fox-hole. Pretty lucky eh? We came out of, or I should say, away from, the front a couple of days ago and we came back here to our bivouac area. We had pup-tents here, sleeping-bags that zipper up the front, a change of clothing and warm food so everything is O.K now. I haven't heard from you since I came overseas but every time the mailman comes I'm right on his neck searching for mail from you. I hear quite regularly from Mum these days and it seems she just received mail from me a little while ago saying I'm overseas. Perhaps that's the reason I'm not hearing from you.

They loaded us in trucks the other day and took us about twenty miles up the road to get shower-baths. Needless to say we needed them real bad. On the way there we came across two Red-Cross women with a truckload of doughnuts. A little while later we went one way with full stomachs and they went the other way with an empty truck. "Those damn soldiers!" I'll bet they were saying..

Now here's a few words your to Mum.

Dear Mum,

Got your Xmas card O.K. Although it was very nice I wouldn't have enjoyed it half so much if it wasn't for the letter you wrote on the inside of it. I haven't heard from Mosher yet but hope to in the near future. I'm glad he got my letter O.K. I often think of that bowl of flowers I got that day and I think:- Gee! I wished I'd known you folks before because you sure were nice to me. (Even if that apple pie was a little sour) Angry? You are? That's good.

Well Mum, my Mum says there are a few parcels heading this way so I'm happy as a lark and my big mouth is watering to beat the devil.

Well, I must close now but thanks a lot for writing, Mum, because a guy can't get too many letters or hear too much about home. And please don't worry too much. And now I switch over to this darn Greta, who seems to have forgotten me entirely and me over here eating my heart out for her.

I hope you've made some Resolutions Greta and that one of them is :- "I will write that homely Peppard boy at least once a week."

Closing for now but my thoughts are ever with you. Write soon.

All my love and kisses

Yours always,
Herbie

P.S :- Postman just arrived with Xmas card from you. I'm happy as can be!

"It was a freezing cold and wet night in the mountains of Italy," Herb says to me as he continues his stories of overseas in his home in Truro. The kettle boils with a high-pitched squeal as he sets little triangles of turkey sandwiches down in front of me.

His blue eyes twinkle in the sun. "Where to begin?" he asks, smiling.

"I'll start with a story about Norm McLeod."

Herb's unit was spread out facing enemy lines. It was their job to be prepared for an enemy attack, which could happen at any moment. They had just taken a hill from the Nazis and were ordered to dig in to confirm their positions. Tonight, shelter meant digging the deepest foxhole possible. Herb decided to share a foxhole with Norm McLeod. There were shells exploding and the men were scared, so they dug the hole as fast as possible. The foxhole became their sanctuary. They were completely soaked, miserable, exhausted and frozen; but in that foxhole they felt safe. Mud and dirt continued to rain down on them as artillery shells exploded. They only had each other for warmth, so they hugged throughout the night. It was the only warmth — and comfort — they had.

As the night stretched on, a mix of rain and snow seeped into the foxhole. Herb and Norm took turns bailing the water out. They would fill their helmets with water and release it outside the hole. Soon they discovered that their helmets would become useful for another sort of bailing: their urine. It was far too dangerous to leave their foxhole to urinate, so they would use the helmet and then pour it out over the rim of the foxhole. Finally, exhaustion set in and the men tried to sleep. All Herb wanted was to forget about the flooded foxhole and drift into sleep. Just when he had nearly fallen asleep, Norm started talking through his chattering teeth. He talked about his life as a soldier, and how he wasn't really meant to be one. Herb couldn't help but think, *who is meant to be a soldier?*

Eventually Herb managed to fall asleep but woke up when he heard an explosion. Shortly after Herb was woken up, Norm started talking again. But he wasn't talking to Herb, he was praying. Herb couldn't believe it. For the two years Herb knew him, Norm was an opinionated atheist.

He had always been a stalwart non-believer and now there he was praying to the very God he insisted did not exist. Norm was notorious for mocking Christians. He would often say, "wake up, you poor bastards! Are you so blinded by faith that you can't see the hypocrisy of it? How can you believe in a God who would let this cruel slaughter go on? I'll tell you this: I will never cower down. I will never pray to a fictitious something or someone that I know does not exist!"

But in that moment, Norm was praying to God and he wasn't asking for a long life, or to be home again - all he wanted was to live through that night to see another day.

Norm's praying made Herb nervous. Here he was, sharing a foxhole with an atheist who was praying, just in case there was a God. It got him thinking; if a shell happened to land in their small foxhole, or even close by, they would be killed instantly. Herb and Norm were both twenty-three years old. Herb thought he would survive the war, but so did those who had been killed. Everyone spoke about what they would do after the war; everyone had plans for the future. Herb's best friends—Smitty, Lieutenant Airth, Private Briddon, and Sergeant McIvor—all spoke of the future and each of them had ended up in a pool of their own blood. Herb thought of these individuals, and how they thought they would live, just like him.

Yet on this cold, awful night Norm was praying to save his life. He was saying things he vowed never to say. He wanted his life spared, just one more day. Until that moment, Herb had never fully believed in the old adage, "there are no atheists in foxholes," but there it was, right before his eyes—a desperate soldier who needed something to believe in.

January 19, 1944: Italy

My Dearest Greta,

Excuse writing paper as it was the best I could borrow on a moment's notice. Hope you won't mind.

I was just thinking of that poem "The Raven" which goes:-

And the Raven never flitting

Still is sitting, still is sitting

Which puts me in mind of myself waiting for your letter:- still waiting for your letter:- still is waiting, still is waiting. I got your Xmas card O.K but for God's sake <u>write</u> or I'll have to fly over and parachute into a certain orchard on Foundry Hill. But please write and if something is wrong we'll patch it up but if we can't patch things up I'll commit suicide. Worst still, I'll join a suicide unit, the Boy Scouts. I've got you scared now.

Well at last censorship is lifted and I can say we're in Italy attached to the American 5th Army. We sailed from the States to Casa Blanca, North Africa, and it's a real pretty place. Most of the buildings are masonry and nearly all of them are white. The people were mostly Arabs and clad in rags and very dirty. They were awful beggars especially the kids asking for Bon-Bons + cigarettes.

We took a train, a small, typical African train. They loaded us into box-cars which said on the side of them (in French of course) Can accommodate 40 men or 8 horses. We had sleeping bags with the zipper up the front so we kept quite warm at night. It was a four day trip. It was beautiful with olive groves and green fields as far as the eye could see. It was entirely different from what I'd expected. I thought Africa was all jungle or all desert. At last we got to Oran where we stayed for about a week then we said farewell to Africa and sailed to Italy. After a little training to get us in shape we were sent up to the front where we fought for a week. Then we came back for a rest. After a rest of a couple of weeks we were sent to the front again and this time for about twenty-six days. Not bad aye? I didn't shave while there so can you picture me on my return. You know Greta, my beard gets <u>red</u> as the devil when it gets long. I'm a handsome brute with three weeks beard, in need of a wash, (water's for drinking up front) and my clothes dirty as Hell. You should have seen me. I got a German rifle I'm going to give Dad when I get home, I also got an entrenching tool, leather belt and bayonet, mess bit, water bottle, two german (not a small "g") German hats. That's the souvenirs I got.

We don't think much of the Italians. All they're after is your money. Buy this, buy that. By-the-way. I'll send you some African money and Italian money. Franc is worth two cents now. (In peace-time it was worth 25 cents). A lire is worth a cent. Note the plain white places on the bills. Hold them up to the light and you'll see faces.

Must close now.

All my love + kisses.

Yours always.
Herbie

"We fought from December 3 to mid January in the mountains around Monte De Cassino, where German soldiers held every mountain," Herb continues.

His unit was successful in defeating the Nazis, thus liberating many villages and towns. Next they were ordered to Anzio Beachhead where the allies were struggling. Herb and his unit departed from the central Italian mountains in mid January and spent two weeks resting in Naples. They were then shipped up the coast and eventually to Anzio Beachhead, which is south of Rome. The German soldiers kept moving north in Italy because the allies kept pushing them in that direction. In Anzio Beachhead the German soldiers had complete control and allies couldn't defeat them, so they called in the First Special Service Force.

The force took their position on the line, along the Mussolini Canal and the nearby village of Borgo Sabotino. There were about 2,000 soldiers fighting during the day and often at night.

Every night, soldiers in pairs stood guard in advance of their lines. The soldiers at the posts communicated with the soldiers along the lines by telephone, Herb explains.

Herb's buddies George Tratt and Jim O'Brien were left to stand guard at the railroad tracks until reinforcement arrived. When Herb left them, they were in a heated argument.

They had been given strict orders to stand guard and not to move, no matter what. Their responsibility was to cover the unit as they advanced by controlling the machine gun. It wasn't long before the German soldiers began firing on the unit. This is when Tratt and O'Brien's argument exploded. Tratt wanted to move forward with the unit, but O'Brien refused to disobey their orders. Tratt yelled at O'Brien, calling him an old woman, demanding that they move to where the action was. O'Brien wouldn't budge. He refused, saying, "no way, our orders were to stay at this post." He won the argument and the machine gun remained in place. They had been so distracted by one another, they didn't notice that the Nazis were surrounding them – until they heard a roaring German tank coming in their direction. A German officer emerged from the tank and ordered Tratt and O'Brien to lay down their weapons. Then a German soldier appeared out of nowhere – pointing his gun towards Tratt, O'Brien, and a few other men. The officer ordered the solider to return to his unit and he marched the prisoners to a compound where the Americans and Canadians, therefore Tratt and O'Brien, were separated.

"George Tratt and I speak regularly on the phone, and he told me all about his experience as a prisoner of war," Herb said as he continued telling his friend's story.

The German soldiers loaded the prisoners of war into the back of a crowded truck where the only thing keeping them from falling out was a three-foot high rail. Tratt was sick and desperately needed to use the washroom, but they were crammed in like sardines. He made the decision to use the washroom. He let his backside hang off the side of the truck and went right there in the middle of Innsbruck, Austria.

The men were brought to a prison camp called Stalag 7A in Germany, where Tratt would spend the next 12 months in crowded barracks. They had no change of clothing, no showers, and little food. Herb remembers Tratt telling him about eating boiled cabbage, turnips, and potatoes.

"They were able to escape because one morning there wasn't a guard in the camp. The guards had fled because Allied soldiers were approaching. Tratt and his buddies were out of there; they started walking and were picked up by an American truck," he tells me.

The night they went missing, all Herb knew was that they were gone. Herb knew their argument had landed the pair in trouble. The German soldiers had captured them.

"I trudged on with deep thoughts of my friends. My best friend, Smitty, was killed, and my closest friends had been captured. I prayed their lives would be spared," he tells me. Deep within his soul he thanked God that he was still alive.

February 24th, 1944, Italy

My Dearest Greta,

> *Just got your letter today dated Feb. 2nd. Boy! It was swell to hear from you. I've been writing and hoping to hear from you for a hell of a long time.*
>
> *The picture was swell Greta and my morale has soared sky-high. I'll eat about six Germans now and it won't put me out a bit.*
>
> *Here it is 10 p.m. and I'm sitting here in an Italian house (our barracks) by the fire-place. I have to keep the fire going for light as we ran out of candles quite some time ago. I'm stripped to the waist and sweating to beat the devil.*
>
> *I can look into the flame and see millions of pictures just like a movie. By-the-way we're going to have a fire-place in our house aren't we? It'll be swell sitting by an open fire-place in the evening and you reading 'Evangeline' to me. I can hear you now. "The little Village of Grand Pre' bay in the fruitful Valley. Vast meadows stretched to the westward giving the valley it's name." It goes something like that doesn't it Greta? I'm glad to hear you like poetry. I can see we're going to get along much better than I thought. If you go to the Library try and get Robert Service's, "Rhymes of a Red Cross Man" you'll like them very much. (That's if you like sad poetry).*
>
> *I got seven letters today. One from you, four from Mum, one from Dad, one from sis Louise. I was happy as the devil I nearly went crazy.*
>
> *Iola tells me she sees you quite often. (She always was lucky). I hear she'll be a mother soon and I'm going to be a proud uncle.*
>
> *My next birthday is July 7th and I'll be 24 years old. Mum tells me I was born discovered one day when a circus came to town. She said she had a boy born to her that day and he crept out to the street and watched the parade. Fifteen minutes later I crawled in and she's kept me ever since. I guess Dad and her had quite an argument as to their opinion whether I'd ever walk on my hind legs or remain on all fours the rest of my life. Who said:- "Honesty is the best policy?" now I've lost my girl-friend just for telling the truth.*

Must close now.

Write soon. Say hello to Mum MacPhee for me.

Thinking of you constantly

All my love

Yours,

Herbie

Despite their elite training, Herb's unit spent 99 days at the Anzio Beachhead. Their plan had been to move as fast as they could travel to Rome, which they hoped would be the first capital city liberated. However, this plan, which they called S.N.A.F.U. (Situation Normal: All Fucked Up), didn't go accordingly.

Herb's unit suffered so many casualties that they couldn't move forward, so they were left with no choice but to wait for reinforcement. The unit was confined for four months on the Anzio Beachhead, where their nights were spent patrolling. They were bombarded by shellfire the entire time.

It was during their time at the Anzio Beachhead that the German soldiers nicknamed Herb's unit the "Black Devils," only later to become known as the infamous Devil's Brigade. They earned this nickname because they painted their faces black with shoe polish and snuck into German camps. Unafraid, they would go right up to sleeping German soldiers and drop off propaganda and notes, hoping to scare them.

The unit was incredibly clandestine. At times they were noticed, but they were never caught.

The FSSF weren't the only ones delivering messages through propaganda. The German soldiers dropped their flyers from the sky.

Lying in his foxhole, Herb stared up at the hills surrounding him. It became obvious to him why their mission had been challenging. The hills surrounding their units were occupied by German soldiers— who watched their every move.

It wasn't until May that they finally broke out of their confines on the Beachhead. The entire unit crossed an open field, suffering a great number of casualties. They came under strong artillery fire and were ordered to wait it out. Herb recognized the sound of the guns as '88.' This particular gun had a destructive and vicious effect on both individuals and aircraft.

As Herb watched shells land around him, he noticed that not every shell exploded. Earlier, Herb had spoken with fellow soldiers about the forced labour being used in German munition plants and about the many Polish labourers who had been forced to work in munition factories. It was rumoured that in order to disrupt the Nazis, they sabotaged some of the artillery shells to prevent them from exploding.

"Thank God for the Polish workers," Herb and his buddies sang as a shell landed nearby without an explosion.

After enduring hours of shelling, a buddy of Herb's — Frank — crawled into his foxhole with him. His face was white as a ghost and his hands were shaking. Frank stuttered over and over that he couldn't stay in his own foxhole, but he wouldn't tell Herb why, so Herb asked to see for himself. The two men crawled on their stomachs fifty yards until they reached Frank's foxhole. Frank pointed to a shiny object extended through the wall of his foxhole: an 88-artillery shell. *Thank God for the Polish workers*, Herb thought again. The shell had hit the ground and pushed through to Frank's foxhole, but miraculously, it didn't explode. Knowing that it would detonate eventually, the men crawled back to Herb's foxhole.

The force had a lot of ground to cover and there were many battles with German soldiers. They pushed the German soldiers back along the Mussolini Canal and other historic villages, like Artena. The head of the force, Colonel Frederick, established his headquarters at strategic locations in the mountains, in historic villages, and in a castle. Colonel Frederick had headquarters in the mountains so that he could have a clear vantage point of the German soldiers. But the Nazi threat continued. He spent many nights wide-awake—on patrol.

Night faded to early morning and thick spring dew settled on the fields. Herb was trudging back to his foxhole after patrolling all night long. He was hungry, cold, and too tired to think. As he trudged through the forest line, his eyes settled on something marvelous. It was a sea of red. Untouched by bombs or the deceased was a field flooded with poppies. He knelt down and picked a poppy. It was the size of his palm, much larger than the ones his father planted at home. Herb closed his eyes and envisioned the field. He wanted to remember it forever.

The allies, including Herb's unit, the FSSF, continued to push the German soldiers out of areas they occupied, liberating towns and villages as they went.

Herb couldn't wait to get to Rome, known as "the Eternal City." His unit had to fight their way there in order to liberate the city, and that's when it happened. It was May 29th, 1944 and Herb's unit had just taken a hill from the Nazis. Many members of the FSSF were severely wounded, including Herb.

He felt a tremendous smash on his right thigh.

"I remember thinking my God, I've been shot," Herb tells me.

"Medic...medic...medic!" Herb yelled from the grass.

"Where ya hit, Pep?" asked George Wright as he crouched down in the grass beside his wounded friend.

Before Herb had time to answer, George was hit in the stomach.

The two friends were left side by side in the dirt.

Eventually, two medics came to their side. Herb couldn't believe how brave they were—entering a battlefield to help the wounded.

"Where are ya hit?" asked a medic as machine gun fire and artillery shells exploded around them.

Two medics patched up his wound, but they had to help the seriously wounded first—so they picked up George.

"We're going to take your buddy first," said one of the medics. Herb laid there and watched the medics load his friend onto a stretcher.

"We'll be back in a couple of hours," one of the medics promised Herb.

Len Anderson, the soldier who replaced Smitty after he was killed, came to Herb's side.

He checked on Herb, and brought him to a nearby foxhole, making sure he was okay before he continued on.

But as he lay on his own, in his foxhole, Herb let his mind wander.

He thought about his friends and family in Truro. Then he thought of his school days, when he experienced an epiphany like none other before.

"They had been preparing us for war when we were little kids! When we were eight and ten years old!" Herb said to himself. Herb thought back to when he was in grade three and four, there was a framed poem on the wall of his classroom. The poem read, "It may be a small bit of bunting / It may be an old coloured rag, / But thousands have died for its honour, / And shed their best blood for the flag!"

Beside the poem was the Union Jack flag. Herb thought back to all of the poems about war he was asked to memorize at such a young age. He remembered reading other poems as well, but they were not encouraged to memorize poems about nature and topics other than war.

He thought about his teachers and the way they taught children about patriotism and self-sacrifice. After learning about Hitler's cruelty, thousands enlisted. Herb believed some credit is due to poems engraved in their impressionable minds.

There he laid alone in a small pool of his own blood, feeling sick. Scared, lonely, and in pain, he laid there in his small foxhole, waiting for anyone to return. He wondered how he could trust that the medics would be back for him. It would mean running the gauntlet of machine gun and mortar fire. Fortunately for Herb, the medics read the same heroic poems — they were back for him and they were heroes now, too.

The medics loaded him into the back of a jeep and drove away from the battlefield, which was just outside the town of Velletri. The next day he woke up in a hospital bed in Anzio Beachhead. The hospital was a large tent with big red crosses painted on the outside to ensure enemies wouldn't attack. Hospitals were safe and sacred places.

He heard moaning and sobbing from wounded men. Many had lost a leg, or worse—both.

Because Herb was left untreated in the grass for hours with his wound, it was infected. His wound wasn't getting any better and they had very little equipment, so he was airlifted to the U.S. army hospital in Naples, where soldiers with critical wounds were taken.

Herb was treated with what soldiers were calling "the wonder drug," also known as Penicillin. He was given an injection of Penicillin every three hours to treat the infection in his leg.

Herb (top right) on crutches in June, 1944

Herb's unit, the First Special Service Force, was the first to enter Rome, the Eternal City, and begin its liberation.

"I was devastated that I couldn't be with them on that historic day because I was still wounded in the hospital," Herb told me.

June 5, 1944: Italy, Hospital in Naples

Dearest Greta,

Well sweetheart guess where I am now? I'm in a hospital between nice clean sheets and I'm getting lots of eats.

Yes my luck ran out at last and a sniper got me through the right leg. The bullet went in the hip and came out the inside of the thigh. It never hit a bone or nerve just injured a few muscles. I have a cast on my leg and around my waist so I cant sit up. (Just trying to apologize for my writing again.) I expect to have the cast removed tomorrow and my wound sewed up.

I will write again tomorrow or next day. If I dream of that homely mug of yours while I'm in the...ether I'll never come to.

All my love
Herbie

June 10th, 1944: Italy, Hospital in Naples

Hello Dearest,

I suppose you got the "v-mail" letter I wrote to you a few days ago. At last, however, I got some airmail envelopes so I can write a longer letter.

Yes sweetheart, at last my luck ran out on me but I shouldn't complain as it could have been much worse and I've been more than lucky up to this time. Incidentally this hospital is much more comfortable than a foxhole.

My only regret is that I never got to see Rome. I was about fifteen miles from the city when I was hit. Damn it! We passed through three Italian towers and the people were all out cheering and clapping. We never even looked at them just kept on going. Quite a few families were living in caves outside the town. They had hardly anything to eat. At last the invasion has started Greta. I know how you and your family must feel but don't worry Mosher will be O.K. He's not dumb like me he'll know how to duck. I hear the 3rd Can division is in there and I'm keeping my fingers crossed for the boys I know in it. I'm awful sorry to miss the "big show" but a soldier usually goes where he's told. Maybe I'll get over to France before it's over.

The only thing I don't like about this hospital is that ever since I was operated on (five days ago, when they took off my cast and sewed my wound up) they've been giving me shots of stuff to keep out infection. The hell of it is they shove the needles in my ____ ____ ___ ___ hip (I'd better not say). I get a shot every three hours. I don't know how much longer it will last but I shouldn't complain as it's for my own good. They took some skin off my other leg for grafting purposes.

How's Mum MacPhee and does she still love me?

I'm just living for the day I get home and hear you sing for me. What's your favorite hymn?

Must close now. I'll write as often as possible but I imagine it will be some time until my mail catches up to me.

All my love

yours always,
Herbie.

July 23, 1944 Italy, Hospital in Naples, Sunday morning 10 o'clock

My Dearest Greta,

Got your letter a couple days ago but I'd just written to you the day before that so I wrote to your Mum. Of course I'm too dumb to be of much comfort to her but I realized how bad she must feel and I had to write something.

I know you must feel bad so I'll have to try and cheer you up. Do you mind?

About you being my nurse. How could you nurse me when I'd be holding your hands all the time and stealing kisses whenever you left an opening? It'd be rather hard wouldn't it? But I know I'd get well much quicker with you as my nurse because I'd just have to walk to show you Naples, Pompeii, and Mt. Vesuvius although I doubt whether I'd be paying any attention to historic sights with you by my side. Glad to hear you're going back to work again and that you're feeling well. After all, we'll need money to go to the movies when I get home. Now I've got you mad again.

Since they put that graft on my leg I'm still a bed-patient and they have splints on my leg so I cant bend it and prevent the graft from healing. I'm in a hell of a shape but I still maintain I <u>will</u> <u>not</u> use the bedpan so I get a fellow to take me to the latrine in a wheel-chair. Did I hear you laugh? You'd better not.

Mum, dad, you and Louise all have hope of me getting home. What's the meaning of that? Do you think a little bullet is going to stop a Peppard? That's a laugh. There's lots of work to be done yet sweetheart and little Herbie is going to be helping them soon. Not that I like war. God forbid!! Anyone that's been in action hates war. It's not your own personal suffering so much. It's seeing the fellows, you've fought with back at camp, ones you've slept with in foxholes, ones you've joked with, marched with, sang with, showed snap-shots to each other; its seeing these fellows blown to bits or shot down in their tracks that makes you hate war, and hate all Germans in general. It's not that I don't want to see you, and hold you, I've dreamed of that many times, its just that I want to stay over here till the war's over and <u>then</u> I'll see you and the folks. Afraid? You're damn right I'm afraid but as soldiers we Canadians have a swell record and a little thing like being afraid is not going to harm that record if we can help it.

And so I've rambled on and likely you're tired of this bull so I'll shut up on that subject. I'm reading a swell book. "How Green was my Valley." I saw the picture twice, (with Mum both times, I didn't have any money), and I read the book once before. If you haven't read it, and you get the chance, you should read it. You'll like it.

One of the fellows took me down stairs to the movie yesterday on a wheel chair. They wanted the wheel chair back upstairs so I got into a chair and saw the show. After the show I looked around but he hadn't come back with the wheel chair and all the hollering I did was to no avail because he didn't come down for another hour. Was I sore! It's nothing to laugh about you devil!

Will close now.

Write <u>soon</u> and <u>often</u>.

Love and kisses and a big hug.

Yours always,
Herbie

From his window, he had a beautiful view of the ocean and the city of Naples. In the distance loomed Mount Vesuvius and the constant cloud of smoke billowing from its peak. Herb was treated well in the hospital. It was warm; he had good food, clean clothes, and doctors and nurses to take care of him.

Five months later, Herb was still in the hospital. He was grateful for movie nights and special events like having American boxers come in and entertain them. After spending five months in the hospital, he really cherished entertainment; it helped his morale.

Herb had six operations on his legs - three on his wounded leg and three on his healthy leg. One of the bigger procedures was grafting skin from his left leg to his right leg.

Sunday, 11:30 a.m. October 1, 1944 Italy Hospital in Naples

My Dearest Greta,

Got your letter last night and what's the big idea: Trying to kick the-bucket behind my back? Have you no consideration for me? Why don't you wait till I get home before you get sick? No, No, I take that back I want to come home to that same big, healthy, beautiful girl, who tried to force more potato scallop on me when I was on a diet. As you noticed I didn't eat as much as a canary would that night. You're a funny girl in a way Greta. I never hear you've been sick till after you're better. And I don't like it. I realize you couldn't write but why didn't you get your Mum to write for you? Of course you couldn't put as much "dirt" in your letter but at least you could let me know you were sick. Don't you think I like to worry about you and say a prayer for you? Although I doubt if "He" would pay much attention to what I'd ask but I could try. I'm real sorry you were sick dear and I hope that "Old Fashioned Flu" stays away from you.

So Louise and family were up to see you eh? Them damn Peppard's will have you in the family before I get home! They'll make terrible "In-Laws" don't you think? And Louise hugged you eh? I like her but when I hear that it makes me jealous as Hell of her.

Bill Kreiser, I don't know him by name but I may know him to see him. And if I do see him and he has a picture of you, and his intentions are honourable, I shall greet him as an unwelcome rival. Thanks! a lot for telling me Greta as it proves to me a thing which I've wondered about for a long while. And don't be afraid to tell me anything like that again as I've told you about myself and of course you're the only one for me from now on.

So Albert's shy is he? That's the way with all us Peppard's. Shy as Hell! Perhaps he'll get over his shyness even if I haven't.

I'm glad you're going to Montreal. It'll be a swell trip for you and I know you'll enjoy yourself. I can just see you shopping at Eaton's and going up on those escalators. You'll enjoy it I'm sure. If you go up on Mount Royal you get a swell view of the city but you can tell me all about it when you get back. I do hope you get a chance to go to Ottawa. It's the nicest city in Canada in my estimation.

So you were all alone that night eh? And no Herbie to squeeze you so hard it'd take the wind out of you. "C'est la guerre." And don't you think I didn't long to be there.

With everything else you have and are a cook also! That's too much! I'll have to hear confirmation of that. So give poor little, innocent Louise a bit of something you've baked and if she continues to write I'll say your cooking's O.K. Agreed? Good! Now one of my favorite dishes is Cod-fish cakes. I love them. Potato scallop is another. Pastry, is date squares, and butter scotch tarts. Enough of this I'm getting hungry again. Now for my condition. I'm so damn tired of talking about it I feel like saying the hell with it and continuing my letter but I'll tell you. I feel swell but I'm still on crutches but my leg's just about healed. The doc said I'd be "A" category and fit for combat when I get out of here. Of course I knew I would be and he just confirmed my belief. You can't keep a good man down.

We had a swell time the other night. "Whitey," next bed to me, sleeps in the nude and I do also you know. (No you wouldn't know what in hell am I talking about) After lights were out I jumped up and pulled the bed clothes off him and threw them on the floor. He said the nurse was coming and he jumps in bed with another fellow so he could cover up. Then I jumped right on top of the both of them (with a blood curdling yell of course.) Just then the door opened and the nurse poked her head in. Boy! did I get back in my bed fast. She must had been afraid to come down and give us hell as she just said, "Be quiet please," then she left. What a relief! And what a laugh we had!

Love to the MacPhee family a big kiss to Mum and lots of Hugs and Kisses to her little daughter Greta.

Love and Kisses,

Yours always,
Herbie

P.S <u>Always thinking of you.</u>

During Herb's last month in the hospital, a man named Perkins moved into the bed beside him. Perkins had been a member of a tank crew and his tank took a direct hit by an anti-tank shell. When a fire exploded inside his tank, Perkins was lucky to make it out alive. He was rushed to the evacuation hospital just in time to save his life before being transferred to the hospital in Naples. Perkins suffered significant burns and his entire face was covered in bandages. Herb and Perkins became friends for the entire month.

They shared stories about their girlfriends at home, whom they each hoped to marry when the war ended. Herb loved talking about Greta.

Perkins was from the United States and lived on a farm with his family, where he hoped to return. The two friends played cribbage, told stories, and had lots of laughs.

Herb waited every day to see if the nurses would remove the bandages from Perkin's face. This whole time there had only been slits for his eyes, nose, and mouth. One day, a nurse came into their room to tell Herb that he would be released the next day. He was elated by the news. Shortly after, Perkins learned that he would have his bandages removed only three days later—Herb couldn't believe he would miss the great reveal. He waited a whole month wondering if his friend was handsome, plain, or ugly, but vowed instead to remember him as a good friend.

Once he was released from the hospital, Herb was sent to a rehabilitation camp where he stayed for a week. He was told his unit had pushed on to Southern France and he was obligated to join them, meaning he might not ever see Rome. Herb visited the commanding officer of the camp and asked for a leave to go to Rome. It was the officer's job to get the soldiers back to their units as soon as possible, so he rejected Herb's request. Instead, he granted him a one-day pass to the nearby town of Caserta, south of Naples, which was considered safe for allies.

Herb decided to go to Rome anyway—Absent Without Leave, once again. He had to see Rome, and he spent a week exploring The Eternal City. Despite being a soldier in a war zone, he acted like a tourist.

He stared in wonder at the miraculous Trevi Fountain. He was mesmerized by the rushing water. He hadn't felt this calm in a while. Leaning over the side he saw coins that had been tossed, and he found himself wanting to make a wish. But he had to continue exploring Rome—he knew he could be arrested at any moment.

He bought a rosary at the Vatican for his eldest sister, Dorothy, and had it blessed.

Finally, he explored the Colosseum. He ran his hand along the archway and then, he got an idea. He picked up a tiny stone and looked around to see if anyone was watching. With his heart pounding, he carved an H and a G. Herb and Greta. He felt satisfied. He was happy that their initials would remain on this ancient battleground for life and he was also happy that he didn't get caught.

Herb loved getting lost in the streets of Rome. He wandered without any plan or intention. He wanted to see everything.

After a week of exploring, Herb felt that it was time for him to return to Naples, find his unit, and join them. Feeling anxious to get back, he stuck his thumb out and waited to see if someone would pick him up.

A British officer with a driver pulled up beside him in no time. The officer called out, "pick up with me!" and Herb got in the backseat of the car with the officer. They were chatting and having a great time all the while; the officer had no idea what outfit Herb belonged to, or that he was AWOL.

Until they stopped at a checkpoint, that is. Military police officers asked to see his pass. He pulled out his one-day pass.

"Come with us," they said sternly.

He said goodbye to the British officer and was promptly arrested.

The police escorted him to a massive transport ship. The ship was full of German prisoners. This is how the military police officers ensured he would return to his unit in Marseilles, Southern France.

He was met by two military police from the First Special Service Force who took him back to his unit.

As soon as he arrived in Southern France, Herb was called in to see Colonel Akehurst.

"Sergeant Peppard, this is a very serious offense!" Colonel Akehurst yelled at Herb.

Herb nodded.

"You put me in a very difficult position. Here you were AWOL in a warzone, yet tomorrow you're going to receive the Silver Star!" Colonel Akehurst said.

The Colonel told Herb he wanted to punish him, but he was unable to do so because the very next day Herb was to parade and receive the Silver Star for bravery in action. Herb felt a sense of relief wash over his entire body. He could not believe that he went AWOL and only received a reprimand, again.

As soon as he stepped outside he threw his hands in the air.

Colonel Frederick, now a General, presented Herb with the Silver Star.

"I couldn't believe it," Herb says sitting across from me at his kitchen table. "You're sure you don't want a cookie? I baked them myself," he says, getting up to retrieve a cookie from a pre-packaged Sobey's container. I want to hear about the Silver Star, I tell him. "Follow me, this way," Herb says proudly, leading me into his office.

"This is my citation." Herb points to a framed certificate on the wall.

For gallantry in action near Borgo Sabotino, Italy on 14 February 1944 while leading a six man patrol far in advance of friendly lines, Staff Sergeant Peppard's patrol was ambushed by a raiding platoon of approximately 40 enemy. In the opening fire all five of his men were wounded, one of them seriously. Staff Sergeant Peppard immediately ordered the four walking wounded to withdraw and warn the commander of the impending raid. He fired his Thompson sub-machine gun to cover the withdrawal of his men, until his weapon was destroyed by an enemy bullet and then threw all his grenades. Noticing an enemy squad moving to outflank him, Staff Sergeant Peppard decided to lift his wounded comrade to his shoulders, then alternately walked and ran 1,200 yards to his own lines. Staff Sergeant Peppard's action not only gave timely warning of an impending enemy attack but his inspiring courage and fearless determination saved the life of a wounded comrade.

"That's what I did to earn the Silver Star."

Shortly after, the FSSF rested along the French Riviera and they were granted passes into Nice, France.

The news came in late November of 1944 that Herb's unit, the First Special Service Force, had disbanded. They were stationed in Menton, France. It was the first time Canadian troops were separated from Americans in the unit.

Herb, second from left, and Len Anderson, Smitty's replacement, far right

Saying goodbye wasn't easy for anyone. They trained and fought side by side for almost two years. They became brothers who trusted one another and shared experiences that no one could imagine.

Herb and the rest of the newly disbanded FSSF Canadians sailed to Naples. He was then sent to Avelleno where the Canadian staging area was located. Herb gathered with other soldiers returning from the hospital and was put through various exercises to help get back into shape before returning to their units. Herb was having a hard time adjusting to his new camp. There were individuals from every Canadian unit, including a lot of French-Canadians. Everyone was dressed differently, some in kilts, others in battle dresses, and some even in overalls. Headgear varied from berets to glengarries and wedge caps, which meant different hat badges; artillery, tank corps, and infantry.

The soldiers loved teasing each other about which part of the country they were from—they called one another herring chokers, frogs, sodbusters, bohunks, and bluenosers. Herb was surprised at the way everyone carried on, but enjoyed it because it only emphasized the very special bond they had as Canadians. During his time in the Canadian staging area, Herb grew immensely proud to be Canadian. He started thinking about war and all of the Canadians who volunteered to cross the seas and fight—not only for Canada, but also for the freedom of other countries like Holland, France, Poland, Norway, and Belgium.

Herb's inspiration was the soldiers of the First World War, fighting for freedom, fighting for the right for all nations to live freely. He was aware that 70,000 Canadians lost their lives fighting for those rights. As he looked around at the other men in his camp, he tried to visualize 70,000 soldiers, but it was very difficult.

Herb thought of soldiers joining hands and standing in a line that stretched from Truro to Halifax, a distance of 100 kilometers. That's what 70,000 soldiers might look like, he thought.

Herb's group of Canadians were given a choice to join any Canadian unit so long as it was in Europe. Herb's heart sank because he was hoping that he would be able to join a unit at home. He returned to the First Canadian Parachute Battalion—his former unit before he joined the FSSF. He joined his old outfit in Belfast, England—he wanted to be with the friends he made earlier on in his training, at the very least.

Despite the fact that he wasn't posted at home, he was happy to be in England; and he proudly accepted a monthly raise from $30 per month to $75.

He couldn't help but think that despite all of his parachute training with the First Canadian Parachute Battalion—and then all of the practice with the FSSF—he never jumped in the war. If he had stayed with the First Canadian Parachute Battalion, he likely would have jumped. Herb learned that his old unit jumped during D-Day and the Battle of Normandy.

He wasn't required to ski, either. The ski training was intended to prepare them for their first mission in Norway, but this mission was cancelled and they were sent to Italy.

May 8, 1945. The war in Europe is over!

We're going home.

"Oh, it was marvelous!" Herb says to me, remembering.

Everyone was hugging, kissing, laughing, and crying tears of joy in the streets.

Herb was in Bulford Camp, England when he heard the long-antic-ipated news. It was Victory in Europe, V-E Day. Herb had to wait over a month before boarding the ship *Isle de France*, in Glasgow, Scotland. There were 8,000 people aboard the ship sailing to Halifax,

Nova Scotia. Every branch of the Canadian Services was there; Army, Air Force, and Navy, including women from each service. Herb met Greta's brother Lloyd MacPhee on board; he served with the North Nova Scotia Highlanders. Herb had heard a rumour circulating that there were riots in Halifax after Victory in Europe Day and they wanted to prevent further riots from happening. So, The First Canadian Parachute Battalion was shipped home. They would be the first complete unit to return to Canada. Their mission was to be an imposing force of soldiers to prevent any more rioting. Herb was happy to be going home.

five

"Humility must be the measure of a
man whose success was bought with
the blood of his subordinates, and paid
for with the lives of his friends."

General Dwight D. Eisenhower, Supreme
Allied Commander, Europe

The ship sailed for days until they finally reached the Halifax harbour. Herb stood at the front of the ship, taking in the familiar surroundings. He saw Citadel Hill and the town clock. More importantly, he felt the salt air on his skin and he smelled wafts of fresh food coming from the local restaurants.

There was a huge crowd waiting when the ship docked in Halifax. As it pulled in closer, Herb saw swarms of people running down the hill toward the ship and lining the dock.

Everyone was waving and cheering.

There was a band playing and people shouting everywhere. Fireboats came out to meet the ship, firing water from their hoses in the air.

Streams of water came down around the ship. The band played "O' Canada," and all of the soldiers broke into tears.

"I felt streams running down my cheeks and I couldn't stop smiling. I remember belting 'O' Canada' and sang along with the band," Herb recounts to me.

When the ship finally docked, the men and women rushed off to see what familiar faces they could find on the crowded wharf. Herb couldn't hold back the huge smile on his face. He didn't expect to see anyone, but when he entered the building at the pier, there was his brother-in-law, Loran Morrison. At 6'2 and two hundred and fifty pounds, he was easy to spot. Herb was ecstatic to see one of his relatives. Loran was a part of the Shore Patrol, similar to military police, but for the Navy.

Finally, Herb was home. They had been given orders to get cleaned up for a parade through Halifax. Herb paraded down Barrington Street toward the Commons. As he looked around, it seemed impossible that he was here. For the first time in his life, he felt like a hero. People crowded the streets, cheering and clapping. The men paraded on until they finally reached the Commons, where they were met by their commanding officer, Colonel Fraser Eadie, who was presented with the key to the city of Halifax by the Lieutenant Governor of Nova Scotia. After the parade, the men were ordered back to the barracks to get their leave for home.

As it turned out, the riots in Halifax had ended before they arrived home. Herb was happy he could tell his mom that he would be home by tomorrow afternoon.

Herb called his mom, who was shocked to hear his voice. There was no way she could have known he was home. Herb listened as his mother's tears seemed to pour through the phone line. He cried with her on the phone.

The very next morning, he boarded the train for Truro. The train was on a milk run, stopping at every station along the way. Herb couldn't wait to get home.

When Herb finally reached the train station in Truro, he searched the crowd eagerly for both his huge family and the girl he had been dreaming about for two years — Greta.

Truro, Nova Scotia in June, 1945

Greta didn't show, and Herb didn't expect her to. It was possible she had found someone else.

Then Herb spotted his family, and all 11 of them walked home together. Herb held his youngest brother Billy's hand the whole way. Billy was nine years old and very proud of his brother. Herb tried to conceal his emotions; having experienced World War Two first hand, he wanted to portray himself as the big, brave soldier.

**The Peppard's: From top: Ray, Iola, Dorothy,
Betty, Louise, Albert. Bottom: Herb, Mrs. Peppard:
Ida, Billy, Mr. Peppard: Herb Sr., Patricia**

The grass was green and the trees were in full bloom. The summer was just beginning and he had made it home. Herb was elated. Entering his house, he was hit with the mouth-watering smell of a roasting chicken coming from his mom's old wood stove.

Herb's father's sanctuary, the garden, was plotted to perfection with each row neatly defined and the tops of crops poking through.

Herb ran through each room of his house. There was the living room, where they would place the Christmas tree, and the spare room where Mrs. Peppard gave birth to almost all of the children. So many memories in this home, he thought. Finally, he was home with his brothers and sisters, mom and dad — where he belonged.

Herb's next task was finding Greta to confront her about how she felt about him. Herb stayed up all night thinking about what she might say. He went through all of the possible reasons she might not want to date him. Number one was his career; it wasn't exactly a stable career and he could be shipped off to fight the Japanese soldiers any day. Would he have enough money to support her?

He shifted from one side to the other. It felt so good to sleep in a bed. If only his mind would rest.

He returned from the war with no trade and no job. It was also likely that she had all kinds of boyfriends. Herb started thinking he was probably overreacting. He wasn't going to ask her to marry him, at least not today; he just wanted a date.

The day after he returned home, he walked down to the telephone office where she worked. He kept repeating a quote to help build confidence: "Most of the things I've worried about never happened."

This helped, but he was still shaking. He was dressed in his freshly ironed army uniform, polished brown jump boots, and maroon beret. He went into the telephone office and knocked on the door. He expected Greta to answer, but it was a man Herb recognized as Ernie. Herb asked for Greta and waited nervously. Greta came out into the small entryway of the telephone office and shut the door behind her. Here they were, so close together.

She is beautiful, Herb thought to himself. She had long, dark brown hair that was gathered at the nape of her neck and at the top of her head. She had sparkling blue eyes. She was wearing a blue skirt and a white blouse. First, they discussed Greta's brother, Mosher, who had been killed overseas. Herb trained with Mosher in the First Canadian Parachute Battalion in Georgia, but when Herb transferred into another unit he never saw Mosher again. Mosher has been a Sergeant and was supposed to have been promoted to Lieutenant the very day he was killed. Mosher was one of the first Canadians in France. He had been handpicked to parachute in the dark the night before D-Day. The First Canadian Parachute Battalion fought for 85 consecutive days. They had cleared out all of the German soldiers, but unbeknownst to them, one lone sniper had remained. He killed Mosher.

Then they talked about Lloyd, another of Greta's brothers. She had five. Her brother Ira MacPhee was also in the North Nova Scotia Highlanders. Herb told her he met Lloyd on the *Isle de France* on their way back to Nova Scotia. On the ship home, Lloyd told Herb all about his experience as a prisoner of war in Germany. Needless to say, Lloyd was anxious to get home. Herb never did mention Greta to Lloyd. He was nervous that nothing would become of their relationship so he kept it to himself. After what seemed like 10 minutes, but was more like 30, Greta had to get back to work.

Herb loved Greta and he didn't want to leave her.

"Will I see you again?" Herb blurted out. He had to ask her before he left. "If you wish," Greta replied.

Herb and Greta outside the telephone office in Truro

That night, Herb and Greta went to a movie at the Royal Theatre. Herb didn't care what was playing, he was just happy to be sitting next to Greta. After the movie, he walked her home and cursed himself for not having enough courage to kiss her.

Herb loved Greta from the moment he saw her and now he couldn't possibly spend enough time with her. They went to the movies, for walks, to the beach. They did everything together. Herb wanted to impress her. One time, his eagerness to impress Greta would get him in trouble.

On one of their romantic walks near the town reservoir – Herb brought along his father's pistol. He wanted to show off. When they reached the woods that surrounded the reservoir, Herb set up a tin can as a target and fired a shot.

Herb watched Greta jump back, and then she wanted to try. Now, he was impressed. Standing behind her and lining the pistol with the target, Herb walked Greta through the motions of shooting. They were laughing and shooting at the can when someone started shouting.

"You're under arrest!" yelled an officer that was running toward them.

Herb was shocked and he knew Greta would be frightened. Luckily he was holding the pistol when the officer approached them.

"For what?" Herb asked.

"For discharging a firearm in a public park!" said the park attendant.

The wooded area where they had been shooting was now a part of Victoria Park.

Herb encouraged Greta to go home while the park officer took him to the Truro jail.

"You're not overseas anymore, Sergeant!" said the Chief of Police, Jack Fraser.

Herb had always admired Jack; he was in good shape and he embodied what Herb had thought of the perfect police officer. But right now Jack wasn't very happy with Herb.

A few days later, Herb appeared in court, but the judge said that because of his war record, they would dismiss the charge. They also returned his dad's pistol.

Herb had a month leave before he would be posted again so he decided to visit his buddy George Tratt in Montreal. He brought his little brother, Billy, along.

Herb's mom, Ida, made Billy a little uniform so he could feel and look like his older brother, whom he admired so much.

Herb fought so long in Europe that he had earned a month off to spend how he'd like before possibly heading overseas to fight the Japanese soldiers.

Billy was only 10 years old and Herb was 25. When they boarded the train little Billy had only $8 in his pocket. Billy played cards with soldiers the whole way to and from Montreal. His mother got a kick out of him when he came in the door with four extra dollars.

Herb and his youngest brother, Billy

While Herb was home, he found out that his friends Freeman and Doug had also survived the war. They both fought on Juno Beach during D-Day in 1944, where 340 Canadians were killed. He was amazed the three of them survived. He imagined that they, like him, experienced vivid flashbacks.

His month at home flew by and now it was time to return to the army.

He joined an army camp in Niagara-on-the-Lake. During his time in Ontario he participated in another wonderful parade, in Toronto. He marched through the streets with his fellow soldiers of the First Canadian Parachute Battalion and enjoyed the same treatment he received in Halifax. Crowds were cheering and one of their Corporals was presented the key to the city. Corporal Frederick Topham was decorated with the Victory Cross, the highest honour a Canadian military person can receive. Colonel Topham earned this honour through his work saving lives as a medical orderly. In the middle of a raging battlefield he would treat the wounded and help bring them to safety. He was even shot in the nose during one of his missions, but continued to help others.

For Herb, the medics in the army were the most brave. These individuals had the difficult task of treating the wounded while under fire. They were not allowed weapons, yet were among the soldiers in the front lines. Herb grew close to two medics who were in the First Company, First Regiment, of the FSSF with him. Shells were exploding, machine guns going off, and these men were in the open. They would patch wounds, give medicine, and make sure those wounded were carried back to the medical officer. When Herb was wounded, frightened, or suffering, a medic would jog up to him and say, "you're going to be OK, buddy."

Or to another soldier, "where have you been hit?" They were always by your side and Herb believed that was the model of bravery.

Following the parade and excitement, the men returned to their camp at Niagara-on-the-Lake. Herb found it more like vacation than work. They swam, played sports, and took leaves to visit Toronto for the day. He knew this would not last. The war was still on, after all. The Japanese soldiers were proving to be a challenging enemy. The soldiers stood prepared to be shipped to the Far East at any moment. Herb heard many things about the Japanese soldiers — that they would die for the Emperor and they welcomed death. This was contrary to the Canadians, who would do anything in their power to stay alive.

It was announced that atomic bombs had been dropped on two cities in Japan. One of these bombs, said to be as powerful as 18,000 tonnes of TNT, was dropped on the city of Hiroshima, killing 135,000 people and leaving the entire city in ruins. The second bomb was dropped on the city of Nagasaki, with a similar outcome, killing an estimated 50,000 people.

It was in the late summer of 1945 when Herb returned home from Niagara, Ontario. He was 25 years old and in very good shape. His first task was going to the Army Depot in Halifax to be "mustered out." This meant he got his army discharge and a mustering-out pay. He was also given a clothing allowance, no longer permitted to wear any army uniforms. He and his buddies stood on Barrington Street looking at each other in their new civilian clothes. After buying his new clothes, Herb headed straight to the railway station. It was time to get back to Truro, to his family, friends, and the woman he wanted to marry. Herb reflected on the first time he met Greta's parents, Nellie and Mosher MacPhee. "We named her Greta, because it means 'Lover of Flowers,'" they told him. He would never forget that.

After spending time with his family and Greta in Truro, Herb realized it was time to find a job. Both his father and Greta suggested he study to become an electrician. Herb studied every weekday at the Vocational School in Halifax. He would be home most weekends, unless he needed some money. Those times, he would stay in Halifax to work at Farmer's Dairy. It involved a lot of manual labour, but luckily he was able to eat all the ice cream he wanted.

Herb and Greta began planning their wedding one year after the war ended. Herb went to Margolians on Inglis Street to buy his suit. The owner at the time was Bernie Sidler.

"What can I do for you?" Mr. Sidler asked.

"I'm looking for a suit for my wedding," Herb said. He was so proud.

Mr. Sidler showed Herb every suit in the store. Herb really didn't know a thing about suits. "I really like the suit you're wearing," he told the dapper owner.

And just like that, Mr. Sidler sold him his suit off his back. Herb smiled from ear-to-ear as he carried home his suit. He thought about Greta, and what she would look like on their wedding day: beautiful, he thought.

Greta made her very own cream suit.

On June 10, 1946, their wedding day, Herb was nervous yet excited. He was 25 years old and Greta 21.

As he washed and dressed and readied himself for their day, he couldn't believe the woman he had written for years would finally accept his hand.

He brushed his hair over and over again. It seemed like no matter how many times he ran his brush through his hair, he couldn't get it to sit right.

"Let me have that brush!" Herb's brother, Ray, said. He had been watching Herb struggle from the hallway.

Ray brushed his hair hard and after trying to get it to look smooth and in place, he gave up and left Herb to his brushing.

He sat on his bed, bending over to tie his shoes. His hands were trembling ever so slightly with the turn of each lace. He thought of the Irving Berlin song lyrics and gently sang them to himself.

I'll be loving you, always

With a love that's true, always

He continued to sing and he felt relaxed. Now it was time to get married.

The wedding took place at the United Church Manse—the minister's home on Queen Street. They couldn't afford a big wedding, but they were ecstatic about finally getting married. Their families had decorated the Manse in beautiful purple lilacs. Herb didn't care that the ceremony was at the Manse, he was just happy to stand beside the most beautiful woman he had ever seen, his soon-to-be wife.

Herb took in a deep breath as he set his eyes on Greta. They stood before the minister in front of an old, beautiful fireplace. The room was filled with the intoxicating smell of lilacs and he felt as though he and Greta, despite being surrounded by friends, were the only people in the room.

The minister instructed Herb and Greta to repeat their vows. Herb couldn't stop stuttering, and he was impressed that Greta hadn't skipped a word.

Then, the minister came to his final words, "As long as you both shall live," and Herb made a silent vow. *My wife, I will love you, protect you, respect you, take care of you, and cherish you as long as we both shall live.*

Herb and Greta were pronounced husband and wife. He knew he was the luckiest man in the world.

After the wedding, Herb and Greta climbed into Tom MacPhee's car; Tom was Greta's youngest brother and Herb's best man. They drove to Roby's Studio to have their pictures taken. Their wedding reception was held at Greta's parents' house, and then it was time for the honeymoon.

Herb and Greta took the train to New York City. They spent five wonderful days taking in the sights and celebrating being husband and wife. But when they returned, Herb's need to find a job became a reality, and there was little work in Truro. That's when Herb called his army buddy, Jim O'Brien. Jim convinced Herb that it was a good idea for him and Greta to move to Bridgeport, Connecticut. Herb was offered one job as an electrician's helper, but they were only offering him thirty-five cents an hour. Herb felt that since he studied electrical work for a year in Halifax, he should be making more.

Herb needed a sponsor to move to the United States, and Jim agreed. Jim didn't have enough money in the bank to qualify as Herb's sponsor, however, so he asked his brother, who successfully sponsored the newlyweds.

It wasn't easy for either Herb or Greta to leave their hometown and their parents, but economically, there were more opportunities south of the border. Herb and Greta were nervous as they boarded the train, leaving Truro behind.

Herb wanted the best for their family—Greta was now pregnant with their first child. Herb and Greta stayed with Jim and his family until they found an apartment—which was a lot more difficult than they expected.

When renters saw that Greta was pregnant, they would often change their mind about renting to them—they didn't want a squealing baby in their building. Eventually they found a place with a young Polish couple. All they had was a bedroom. They shared the bathroom and kitchen with the other couple.

Herb got a job with General Electric where he worked on television sets on an assembly line. At General Electric, Herb made $1.09 an hour, which was an impressive wage during that time. He couldn't believe his first paycheck: $42.18. He thought he was going to be rich.

Herb also worked for a company called Bead-Chain. At Bead-Chain, they made the chains attached to the rubber stoppers for bathtubs. He also had a job at a rubber factory.

Not long after establishing themselves in Bridgeport, it was time for Greta to have their baby.

Herb worried about Greta in the delivery room. He wasn't allowed in and her mom was far away in Nova Scotia.

Herb watched as nuns walked swiftly up and down the corridor in the hospital where he waited, anxiously.

At 2:00 a.m., nearly seven hours after Greta was admitted to the hospital, the baby arrived. He was red and wrinkled. Herb asked a Sister if this was normal. The Sister assured him that all babies look like that when they are first born. As planned, they named him Herbie, after his father, grandfather, and great grandfather.

Leaving the hospital, baby in his arms, Herb felt extraordinary. He imagined what his little man was thinking. He imagined his baby wondered who this big man staring at him was.

They were on their way home, now a family of three.

At seven months, Herbie was starting to crawl, and he loved looking at himself in the mirror on the bedroom door. When he could finally stand, he stood in front of the mirror, knees shaking, and stared at his little friend in the mirror.

One evening Greta and Herb were playing with Herbie when the telephone rang. Herb assumed it was one of their friends—they had a great social life in Bridgeport, with lots of friends who also had young children.

The call wasn't from a friend. It was for Greta. Her eldest brother, Fulton, only 32-years-old, died from a sudden heart attack, leaving his wife and kids in shock. Greta packed her bags and took Herbie with her to Truro for three weeks. Herb stayed in Bridgeport to work, Greta wouldn't be gone for too long.

Herb was surprised by how lonely he felt without his wife and son by his side. He missed Herbie's little giggles and gurgles. One particular evening, something caught his eye. It was the mirror that Herbie loved; his little handprints were smudged against the bottom of the mirror.

Greta and Herbie at the beach

They had been living in the United States for two and a half years when Greta became pregnant with their second child.

She was starting to feel homesick and wanted to have their second child in Nova Scotia, so they decided to move home. When they reached Truro they couldn't believe they'd ever left. He was always so proud to be Canadian, and Canada would always be their home. They moved into a home on Lyman Street across from Greta's parents. Herb found work at the Truro Train Station Express office, moving shipments on and off trains.

Herb and Greta were happy to be home in Truro. They enjoyed walking to the movie theatre and singing in the park.

One night as they were walking home from the theatre, Greta stopped and stared into the starry sky.

"When we have a daughter, let's call her Lark," she said.

Lark was the name of the protagonist in the film they had just watched. It was the first time Herb or Greta heard the name.

"Lark."

A few months later, Lark was born.

Lark was born in a big, old house on Queen Street, known as the hospital annex—wards were set up to help with patients in the house because the regular hospital was crowded.

The new parents couldn't wait to take their joyful and beautiful baby girl home and begin living as a family of four.

Herb, Greta, Herbie, and Lark

six

"The way to love anything is to realize it may be lost."

G.K. Chesterton

"Yes and good talking to you too, dear," Herb says, hanging up the phone that is strung from a long cord, just reaching him in his wheel-chair. Here he is, in a pale, small but comfortable room, larger than life and still with so much cheer.

"Hello!" Herb says with a smile and open arms. I lean over to give him a hug. It is strange to see him in a wheelchair. Herb fell in his home in the fall of 2012 and is being treated in the veteran's unit of the Queen Elizabeth II Hospital in Halifax. Unlike most who may feel sad and lonely in a hospital, Herb spends his time telling stories and sharing laughs.

"Oh and you brought some treats too, aren't you so kind." His voice bellows. I open a bag of homemade tea biscuits and jam on the desk beside him.

"This is so lovely," he says.

"You know, I'm always injuring my right leg," he says. Herb tells me about how he broke his right leg skiing when he was training for war, about being shot in the same leg and now after this fall, he has a hairline fracture. The hardest times he spent in a hospital were not nursing his own injuries or illnesses, but his wife Greta's.

"It was a crisp evening in late October, it would have been 1952."

"We were walking up Lyman Street, heading home after a night out to the movies."

As they walked up the steep street, Greta gasped for air and couldn't catch her breath. This wasn't normal. When they reached home, Herb called their doctor.

When Dr. Little arrived, he took one look at Greta and called the ambulance to take her to the Truro hospital.

"I watched Greta say goodbye to our kids, eighteen-month old Lark and four-year-old Herbie, not knowing if she would see them again," he tells me.

Poliomyelitis, more commonly known as polio, is a disease that destroys cells in the spinal cord. These cells are responsible for directing signals from the brain to muscles. These signals tell muscles to contract and relax. The disease is selective; polio can destroy muscles, take out a limb entirely, or disrupt breathing and swallowing.

Nova Scotia was not prepared for the polio epidemic. Without the donation of 14 artificial lungs by an English nobleman, many victims would have died. If the victim does survive, the areas affected by the disease are compromised; they may not function the way they did before infection.

"I hate to tell you this Herb, but your wife has polio," said Dr. Little.

Herb could barely see Dr. Little through his tears. He felt his world turn upside down. He was speechless. Greta was so strong and healthy. Polio was the disease that killed people. He was terrified of what could happen to his wife and couldn't bear to think about it.

Almost immediately after arriving at the Truro hospital, Greta was taken to the polio clinic in Halifax by ambulance.

When they reached the clinic, Greta was quickly undressed and given only a sheer sheet. The sheet kept slipping and she was struggling to cover herself but didn't have the strength. She was immediately put into an iron lung.

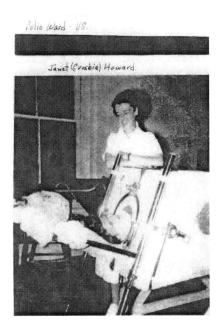

Greta in an iron lung

Herb was overwhelmed by the polio clinic. He was overwhelmed by the number of patients, and that the 'clinic' itself was an army Quonset hut—a portable army building. There was no room in the main hospital, so polio patients were treated in this special, temporary building. This way, the patients with polio were quarantined. The truth immediately hit Herb that there weren't just a few isolated cases; Polio was a full-blown epidemic. The scene reminded him of an army hospital in Italy, overflowing with patients.

"I stayed by Greta's side for an entire month, leaving only to sleep on a gurney in the hall," Herb told me.

He prayed Greta would receive immediate care. Herb was met by a ward-boy nicknamed "Fleegle Eye" because his eyes never stood still. Herb relied on Fleegle Eye for updates on Greta.

"We just put her in the iron lung," said Fleegle Eye. Herb looked at him in disbelief.

"What does that mean?" Herb asked.

He was convinced it would be Greta's love and courage that would determine whether she would leave the hospital alive, not the expertise of the doctors and nurses.

Herb stood beside the iron lung with Greta inside. Greta, his precious and beautiful wife—the woman he had longed to be with for his whole life. Herb thought that the iron lung resembled a coffin in more ways than one. All he could see was her head sticking out of the top. Her body was paralyzed from the waist up; the iron lung was breathing for her.

With Greta confined to the hospital and Herb busy working on the railroad, 100 kilometers away in Truro, Greta's parents cared for Herbie while Herb's parents looked after Lark. The iron lung breathing for Greta was a blessing and a curse: it was keeping her alive, but also keeping her away from her family.

All Herb wanted to do was take Greta home from the hospital, hold her, and tell her he loved her. He was always saying to himself, "Greta, don't leave me. I need you and your love. I don't want to go on without you."

On the outside, he was smiling, saying, "I love you, and everything will be all right."

Nothing could have prepared Herb for the emotions he was experiencing. Why was this happening to such a *good soul?* They had only had been married for five years. They had two young children — and Greta was only 26.

Herb thought about their family. They were a typical young family. Just starting out. Not a lot of money, but they had a lot of love and Greta was a wonderful mother.

With their grandparents looking after Herbie and Lark, and Herb caring less and less about his job at the railroad because of Greta, he spent almost every waking moment at the hospital. Worrying about Greta consumed his life. He was so grateful for his parents and Greta's parents, and for his friends at the railroad who took his shifts at Greta's most critical time. Eventually they were working for him fulltime for an entire month, and giving him his pay.

For the first month Greta was in the hospital, Herb stayed with her every night. Each night, he talked and sang to her.

Some of Herb's nights at the hospital were eerie; It was hard to sleep while listening to the iron lungs. They sounded like bellows making strange swooshing sounds, yet they were keeping Greta, and several other patients, alive. Herb prayed on stormy nights that the power wouldn't fail— if it did, the lungs would also.

One treatment made Herb particularly nervous. The nurses would apply hot packs on Greta's muscles to ease the pain, preventing painful spasms. The nurses would pull Greta from the iron lung, slap on the hot packs, and shove her back in as quickly as possible. She couldn't breathe without the iron lung, and Herb felt the nurses should move faster. It made him sweat every time. He also disliked the look of all of the tubes inserted in different parts of her body, worried about what would happen if one got pulled out accidentally.

As Herb spent more time in the hospital, he grew more alarmed by what was happening around him. There were so many children. He empathized with them — they must have been so scared.

Herb heard that Tatamagouche had also been badly affected by the epidemic. There were thirteen cases of paralysis. Forty percent of residents had polio symptoms. Patients were paralyzed and dying despite the doctors' best efforts. Hearing more tragic stories about polio only made Herb more conscious and more fearful of Greta's condition.

Herb was sitting in the hall one morning when one of Greta's doctors approached him.

"We have to put a tube down your wife's throat. It will ensure that air will reach her lungs if we pull her out of the iron lung for any length of time. We want to be able to hook her up and give her oxygen," the doctor said.

He explained that the procedure could damage her vocal chords, and she may never be able to speak again as a result. Herb agonized over the decision to allow the doctors to proceed with the operation. Was this torture ever going to end, he wondered. He knew he didn't have much time, or choice, and with shaking hands he signed the permission papers.

Eventually, Greta's condition began to stabilize. They watched movies that were projected onto the ceiling. Herb watched many movies with Greta, her wardmates and their family members, but it would always leave him with a terrible pain in his neck. One night, Greta told Herb he had better go home, go back to work, and take care of their children. He was against the idea, but he saw something in Greta's eyes that he hadn't since she became sick. It was determination. She was going to get well. Herb made sure that he was by her side; he wouldn't have had it any other way.

The polio clinic did not have many visitors because everyone was terrified of contracting the disease. Herb brought along his mother, his sister Louise, and Lark for a special visit — Lark's second birthday. Greta was so happy to see her little girl for the first time since she'd fallen ill almost five months earlier.

Greta faced many challenges throughout her sickness and Herb experienced these challenges along with her. During her recovery, the nurses would pull her out of the iron lung for a few seconds at a time and then shove her back in again. Greta's goal was to breathe on her own and return to her family.

Seconds turned into minutes and after a while, Greta no longer depended on the iron lung. Eventually she was lying in a regular hospital bed, breathing on her own. She was terrified to go to sleep, fearful that she would lose her breath. Once she'd accomplished breathing, the next challenge was sitting up on her own. Sitting up after so long would make the blood to rush to her brain, causing her to pass out. After multiple tries, she achieved her goal.

Herb and Greta celebrated their sixth wedding anniversary on June 10, 1952. Greta was still confined to the polio clinic, but with permission from her doctors, Herb was able to take her out for supper to the Sword and Anchor, a local hotel. They shared a meal and then went to the room Herb rented. A big bouquet of flowers Herb bought was on the nightstand. It had been eight months since they had been together and for Herb, it felt like an eternity.

Herb helped his frail wife undress before going to bed. He held her in his arms.

According to her physician, Dr. H. Gordon Quigley, Greta's paralysis affected her upper torso and she had relative movement of her legs. Only months before the couple's dinner at the Sword and Anchor, Herb and Greta communicated by blinking; she would answer "yes," by blinking once and "no" by blinking twice. She was so weak. She was able to use this blinking method because she could still hear, see, and think. Swallowing is an involuntary action that is often affected by polio, and in Greta's case, she was able to swallow, but at the peak of her illness, she was not able to swallow enough to keep her airway free from saliva.

Dr. Quigley had told Herb, "Mrs. Peppard was as near death as she could be." Dr. Quigley didn't have a lot of experience at the time and felt he should know more about her condition. Before too long, he found himself operating an artificial lung and giving Greta an endotracheal tube to help her swallow. He manually ventilated her using a mixture of oxygen and helium. Greta's lips went from blue to red and her cheeks from grey to rosy. Greta was one of the most severe polio cases in Nova Scotia.

After eight months in hospital, Greta Peppard survived polio.

"Through the entirety of Greta's illness, I knew in my heart that my wife would not die," he tells me in his own hospital room. He thought of her as a mother tiger defending her young, which is exactly what she was doing: fighting for her life so she could raise her children.

seven

"Hope springs eternal in the human breast."

Alexander Pope

One month after their sixth anniversary, Greta went home.

The day Greta arrived was full of anticipation and excitement. Herb's parents, Greta's parents, five-year-old Herbie, and two-year-old Lark were all waiting for her. Greta had been fighting for her life and now here she was in her mother's home. Herb saw the joy in Greta's eyes when her two children rushed toward her. But as they came in for her embrace, the reality and horror of polio hit her once again. She couldn't hug them. She was paralyzed from her waist to her shoulders. She desperately wanted to hug her children, but her arms fell limp at her sides.

Greta's mother thought it would be best if she and Herb move into the apartment above their home, and the couple agreed. While everyone was elated that Greta was home, it was apparent that Greta's sickness left her temporarily helpless and with great challenges ahead. Greta depended on her family to help her with even the smallest tasks.

Tasks that Herb took for granted were nearly impossible for Greta. He did everything for her, including pinning sanitary napkins to her underwear, which was initially very awkward for Herb. Soon Herb became her arms and her hands. Greta's mom cared for her while Herb was working, and they hired housekeepers when Greta's mom wasn't around.

Herbie Jr. lived below with Greta's parents and Lark lived with Herb's parents a block away on Alice Street, for the time being.

"Her arms and hands were paralyzed, but that had no affect on her thinking power," Herb tells me.

Shortly after she returned home, Greta travelled to a rehabilitation center in New York City. When she returned two months later, Herb saw a whole new woman. She learned all kinds of coping techniques, such as how to maneuver items without the use of her arms and hands. She opened drawers with her toes and she was given kitchen utensils with rings in which she inserted her fingers, operating as grips. She ran their house the best she could, and Herb admired her courage and determination.

Now that Greta had tools to help her around the house, the children joined she and Herb in the second floor apartment above her parents' home.

Greta became pregnant two more times, but her body was very weak; she lost both babies. Herb knew the miscarriages were really hard on Greta. She was both physically and emotionally exhausted. He knew how badly Greta wanted another child, in spite of her mother's wishes. Nellie MacPhee felt that Greta wasn't strong enough and urged Greta not to have any more children. But she was determined.

Lark was seven years old and Herbie 10 when they met their new baby sister. Herb and Greta welcomed their miracle baby.

Herb and Greta poured through "name" books and the only name they could agree on was "Rosalie." Greta told Herb that she didn't want her daughter's name to end in a "lie," and so they named her Rosalee.

Lark wanted to help her mom as much as she could and she became a strong sister for little Rosalee and helping hands for Greta. Herb was proud of Lark; here she was, so young, a second mom to her baby sister.

Even though Greta had physical challenges, it didn't stop her from going on camping trips and vacations with her family. They went on great adventures. Herb was amazed by the way Greta was able to keep up physically with the rest of the family. She would pick up a plate by sliding it to the back of one hand while steadying it with the back of the other. She taught herself how to perform the same tasks as her family.

One evening, Greta asked Herb if he could share some stories of the war with her.

"You have told me some things about the war, but never about the horrors," Greta said.

She hoped that if Herb shared some of his horror stories, it might unburden him of the memories and thoughts. He told her about the time he carried a legless, armless, headless corpse down the mountain and the terror of seeing the corpse. After telling her the story, he did not feel unburdened; he could not escape such a memory. He began shaking and he couldn't stop. He laid down in his bedroom until he finally stopped shaking. He hated that Greta had seen him so upset, but she was nothing but supportive and loving to him.

Greta and Herb started to build their dream house on a quiet, dead end street in Truro. They had been living on the top floor of Greta's parents home since she was discharged from the polio clinic in 1952 and it was time to build their own home and make new memories.

MacKay Court was named after the MacKay family who owned a lot of property on the street. Herb and Greta spent $750.00 for their lot, which they thought was too much money at the time. However, they had the perfect view of Truro. They built their house exactly how they wanted — a ranch-style brick home, with a matching brick fireplace and a raised marble hearth. Herb wanted to make things as easy on Greta as possible, so their doors had lever handles instead of knobs. They designed their kitchen with a built-in wall oven, and counters at different heights so it would be easier for Greta to use.

In December 1960, the Peppard family left the MacPhee home and moved into their dream home just a few blocks away.

Herb's career as an electrical contractor began to take off. Many young couples were building new homes in the Truro area. He was very busy wiring new houses, running his business out of their home with Greta's help, and continuing to work on the railroad unloading boxes. This meant that he worked eight hours during the day and eight hours at night.

The three children were happy in their new home. They enjoyed playing with other kids in their neighbourhood. Herbie was active in sports such as baseball and track-and-field. He also belonged to several clubs at school. Lark loved to sew and sing. She was part of a folk group, 'The Happy Folk,' along with three of her musical girl-friends. Like her mother Greta, Lark took singing lessons from Helen K. Embree. Rosalee started her musical life studying with the same teacher. Rosalee's beginnings in music, singing, and poetry started in the creative environment of her family's new home.

One evening, while Herb was working the night shift at the railroad, his mind wandered back to when he worked in the lumberyard and lifted weights in the evening—the magnificent barbell. He thought about the way it slid through his hands. Back then he was so strong. The weightlifting club hadn't started up again after the war.

He wanted to rediscover his passion, and be as strong as he possibly could. Herb set up a gym with barbells and dumbbells in the basement. People from all over town would come by to work out with Herb. There were regulars, and Herb Jr. worked out with them as well. It was a very popular spot for many young men in town, especially for policemen and fitness enthusiasts.

They enjoyed their home on MacKay court for 10 years. Herb and Greta raised their kids there. They hosted family parties there. They watched their kids grow up. Herbie and Lark graduated high school and followed their passions. Rosalee grew from a precious three-year-old to a vibrant teenager attending junior high.

Herbie attended Acadia University and graduated with a Bachelor of Arts in English and literature. He then went on to study at York University.

He fell in love with a woman named Judy Hunt. Judy was from Newfoundland and Labrador and they shared a sense of adventure. They travelled to Japan and studied culture together, and had two children. Then they moved to Australia, where in the late 70s, Herbie used his talents to develop a groundbreaking computer program to teach English to Australian immigrants. He won an Australian Education Award for his program. After separating from Judy, Herb Jr. won the heart of an Aussie lady, Deborah Chadwick, whom he married. He went on to have a diverse international career including, creative director for his own company.

Lark pursued her passion of clothing and design. Herb remembered that Lark would go through her mom's closet, looking for dresses she no longer wore, and would make new dresses from them. For Lark's 12th birthday, her grandfather Mosher MacPhee (Sr.), Greta's dad, gave her a portable Singer sewing machine. As a teenager, Lark made her friends' prom dresses.

Her first job was at Martha Murray's Fine Fabrics store in Truro. The owner asked Lark to work for her after school and on weekends. After a year of studying at the Nova Scotia College of Art & Design in Halifax, she returned home and opened 'The Lark Boutique', stocking it with her original clothing designs.

She worked in the creative team for the costume department of the National Arts Center, building garments for plays and operas. Later she worked in two couturier houses, also in Ottawa—one specializing in diplomats' finery and the other creating high quality silk wedding gowns. She married Carmen Hewer, also from Truro, and they have three children.

When Herb was offered a position as an electrical construction wiring instructor at the Vocational School in Bridgewater, he thought about it. After careful consideration and discussions with Greta and Rosalee— who was still just a teen — they moved to Bridgewater.

One year later, the couple bought a beautiful 180-year-old house in Mill Village.

Rosalee thrived in her new high school in nearby Liverpool. She made new friends, many creative and musical like her. She was active in musical plays and was part of a 9-girl singing group, 'The Triple Trio'. They toured and even recorded an album, all while still in high school.

Rosalee graduated from Mount Allison University in Sackville, N.B. with a Bachelor of Music. She also studied at the Banff School of Fine Arts. Rosalee married Allan Lockyer from Newfoundland and Labrador, whom she met in Toronto and they have two boys.

Rosalee has developed her musical career as a unique performer— as a singer, songwriter, and historian. She researches the lives of Maritime and Canadian women and crafts their stories into song.

Despite the fact that he was getting older, Herb decided it was time to start training for bodybuilding competitions.

Herb explained that bodybuilding seemed healthier than weightlifting because he wasn't trying to outlift himself all the time.

"Greta, I'm home and I have some exciting news," Herb sang as he made his way into the house.

Herb told his wife all about the revelation he had had at work.

She encouraged him and said she would help him in any way she could.

He worked out three times a week.

Herb believed that bodybuilding emphasized the importance of exercising all parts of the body.

There were some elements of the sport that made him nervous.

How would he look under floodlights? How did he pose? It was also important for him to be tanned. He was grateful for Greta's help.

Herb was 55 when he participated in his first competition.

Herb was in the bathroom shaving his body. The guidelines of the competition suggested that competitors looked best hairless and tanned.

He twisted and turned, struggling to reach areas on his back that he'd never tried to reach before.

"Greta!" he yelled. She poked her head into the bathroom: he didn't realize she was waiting just outside the door.

"Can you help?" he asked.

With her own technique she squeezed the razor handle between the backs of her hands. In her own way and using much of her body, she shaved the areas that he couldn't reach.

He felt repeated strokes on his back as she tried a few times to pick up every last hair.

When she finished, she sat on the toilet seat and stared at her husband.

They didn't speak.

Herb reached for tanning paint and started rubbing it all over his body. Without having to ask, Greta, again in her own way, tried her best to help paint his tan.

Now, he was ready.

"Herb, do you have everything?" Greta asked.

He had tried his best not to consume any food or liquids the night before to ensure that he would look his best on stage.

"Yes—yes, let's go."

Herb had waited for this day for quite awhile. Bodybuilding still wasn't very popular and this was the first competition of its kind in Nova Scotia. When they reached the YMCA in Halifax where the competition was held, Herb felt similar to the time he was on a ship—seasick.

"It's just the nerves, honey. You'll be fine," said Greta.

He wondered how she knew how he felt without even asking.

Herb watched Greta take her seat at one end of the gymnasium while he lined up with 19 other competitors. He was pleasantly surprised to see the diversity in size and age. However, he wasn't too happy to be standing beside a 24-year-old. He thought about his beautiful wife in the crowd—that was enough motivation for him to try and do his best.

"Herbert Peppard," the announcer barked.

He stepped forward from the line and went through all of the motions he had practiced with Greta. There were floodlights at his feet lighting up his muscles. He felt undressed, and he had no idea what he looked like. At the end of his routine he returned to his place in line and watched on as his competition went through the same motions.

He couldn't help but see that some of the men had a lot of grace—he wanted that too. When the announcer finally called out the winners he was far from the top.

That evening, Herb and Greta fell asleep on the train back to Truro. Herb's head rested against the cold glass, with Greta's on his shoulder.

From that day on, Greta helped Herb with all of his bodybuilding competitions. She shaved his body and applied his tan.

Bodybuilding became Herb's way of maintaining his health and Greta helped him look his best.

"Greta! Could you give me a hand upstairs?" Herb yelled.

It was a dull, fall day and he was upstairs in their house in Mill Village. He had been doing some electrical work that day, which was nothing new. He enjoyed his new job as a teacher, but the work continued at home. While Herb worked away in his old house, he thought of the old times, and what he would rather be doing on his day off. Then it occurred to him that making love would be the answer. He stripped down to nothing but his tool belt and stood at the top of the stairs.

"Greta!" He yelled. "Greta, come upstairs and give me a hand!" Greta often helped him around the house, so he knew she would be along.

His excitement grew as he heard her move from the kitchen to the stairs. He saw her coming up the stairs and then she looked up, delighted and surprised.

"There's a picture that will never be erased from my mind's eye if I live to be 100 years old," Herb said, looking at her expression.

They started laughing and laid down face to face with their arms around each other. In that moment, there was nobody else in the world, no one outside those four walls. Herb knew that nothing would ever come between him and Greta.

"You're crazy, you know that? What if one of our neighbours walked in while you were standing there like that?" Greta said, smiling.

"My God, I never thought of that," Herb said.

"What would our children think of us?" Greta whispered.

"I'm sure they would be really happy for us, and without our love they wouldn't exist," Herb said.

"What would our grandchildren think of us?" Greta whispered again.

"They're too young to understand, but they'd never think of it, of their grandmother and grandfather."

"It's strange dear, but I don't feel old," Greta said.

"You don't feel old at 57, and I don't feel old at 62. We'll continue to love like this forever," Herb said.

"What a wonderful dream, sweetheart," Greta murmured.

As Herb looked at his wife's beautiful face, he knew how lucky he was to have won the heart of such a woman.

His memory took him back to that "day of joy and excitement," when they stood before Reverend Earl Gordon and repeated their wedding vows. That happy day was thirty-six years before.

When Herb's mother passed away, he and Greta bought his childhood home from the family estate. They moved into the very house on Alice Street where Herb was born.

Despite turning 68, Herb continued to weight train and wanted to challenge himself with another competition. Greta coached him the whole way.

This time, he was training for the Nova Scotia Masters, a competition that he had won five years earlier. He knew he could do it again.

He reached center stage and waited for his posing music to start, but couldn't help ask himself, *What the hell am I doing here*? He wasn't in his fifties anymore and he wasn't at the YMCA, either.

This competition was held at The Rebecca Cohen—a beautiful theatre in Halifax.

He glanced at his skin. It still held the perfect tan that Greta had painted earlier. She was in the audience and Herb wondered what she was thinking.

He wanted to make her proud. The music started and he went through each pose with ease. He felt like he was gliding through each motion. The bright lights blinded him from the audience and he was warm. He was in his element and didn't want it to end.

The music stopped and he stepped aside, grinning ear-to-ear.

He won first place in the Nova Scotia Master division.

"My coach deserves all the credit," Herb says with a huge grin. He could talk about her all day.

eight

"Death ends a life, not a relationship."

This is what Jack Lemmon told his friend as he wished him goodbye. This is also the way Herb felt about Greta.

It was a miracle that Greta survived polio and was able to live the fulfilling life she did. Regardless of her physical restrictions, Greta was a strong mother. She never complained, and tried her very hardest not to let her limitations hold her back. She was blessed with a loving husband with whom she never fought, and three beautiful, healthy children.

"Greta was 67, and I was 72 when we travelled to Helena, Montana, for a First Special Service Force reunion," Herb tells me. Now, six months after his first day in the hospital, Herb is back home in Truro.

On their way to the reunion, they stopped in Ottawa to visit Lark, and then took a military Hercules aircraft from Ottawa to Montana. As they made their way through the airport and to the hotel, Herb noticed that Greta was quiet.

She told Herb that she wasn't feeling well, so they laid down to rest before the banquet dinner.

Herb woke up and glanced at the clock on the nightstand. It was 4:15 p.m. He rubbed his eyes and headed for the washroom. He wanted to let Greta rest a few more minutes.

Hot water rushed on Herb in the shower and jolted him awake. He thought about Greta and he wanted her to enjoy herself this weekend. Despite having attended many FSSF reunions, it was likely Greta would meet even more of Herb's buddies from the force this time.

He toweled off and made his way over to his wife, gently nudging her awake.

"What time is it?" she asked.

It was 4:30 p.m., and they were expected in the hall at 5:00 p.m.

Herb knew that she would be a bit upset that he didn't wake her earlier, so she could get ready for the evening.

He helped Greta out of bed and led her to the bathroom. Herb watched her grimace at the lights. Hotel lighting always seemed so unflattering, he remembered her saying another time. But to him she looked no different under the harsh lights.

Soon after getting dressed and sipping on tea in their room, the couple joined their friends at the banquet dinner.

The reunion committee had planned excursions for the force, but Greta wasn't well. They relaxed at the hotel instead, and Herb was happy that he and Greta were able to meet with a lot of buddies he had served with overseas.

On the morning of their departure, Herb and Greta boarded the military jet that would take them home.

The engines rumbled with a start and Herb looked at his wife, still so beautiful. He was worried about her.

Within the first five minutes of flight he knew it was too rough for Greta.

"It was very rough and an officer came in and said Greta could sit with the pilots where it was more comfortable. We went up there together and Greta laid down on my leg and tried to fall asleep," Herb tells me.

He did everything he could to comfort her on their flight home.

Herb felt relieved when they finally reached their Alice Street home. He ushered Greta in with his arm around her.

But she wasn't getting better.

One night, less than a week after returning home, Greta was standing in her housecoat in their living room when she asked Herb to take her to the hospital.

Herb knew how particular Greta was about the way she dressed so he knew it was bad if she wanted to leave in her housecoat. He took her to the hospital and she died the next night. A minister came in and said a prayer. Post-polio syndrome had made her body too weak to continue.

Herb was 72 when he lost the love of his life.

"We were married 46 years. I never cheated on my wife. I never thought about cheating on my wife. I loved her too much for that," Herb wrote in his notebook about Greta's illness.

"I feel I was very fortunate to get a woman like Greta," he wrote.

Herb truly learned about courage and how to love from his wife. He was the muscle but she had the strength.

"I had a hard time figuring out how to live without her."

Greta was the one who organized family gatherings and parties, and she was always calling their kids. "I wasn't good on the phone," he says. She was the glue that held everyone together.

nine

> "There are two times a person notices that they are alone; when they are eating and in bed."
>
> Herb Peppard

He didn't want to carry on. She was his sweetheart.

He tried to think about how lucky he was to have had her for so long. He could have lost her when she was only 26.

"Everyone was telling me the same thing —'get out of the house,'" he says, remembering.

Herb took his friends' and family's advice and joined Toastmasters, a class that taught public speaking. In preparation for his Ice-Breaker speech, he wrote eight pages. Finally, the day came when he would speak in front of an audience. His hands trembled and one page fell to the floor. When he bent over to pick up the fallen page, he hit his head on the lectern. He asked himself, *what am I doing here?* He missed her.

Herb was no stranger to taking risks. He has written in his notes, "I realized, a person must take risks, must challenge themselves or they're doomed for a life of stagnation."

Herb's speeches were stories that he wrote about the war. After telling many of these stories, he was approached by a young woman who suggested he write them down. She had a relative who worked for Nimbus Publishing and suggested that he send them his stories.

Toastmasters helped prepare Herb for years of speaking engagements — in schools, legions, youth groups, leadership programs, the Truro Rotary Club, the Lions Club, and more. Everyone wanted to hear what he had to say: what happened in the war? What did he do? What did he see?

He wondered what people thought of his talks, which often included song, as well.

Herb also wondered what high school students thought of him. Often they hid their cellphones under their desks — sneaking texts now and then. He thought this was something they liked to do. Teachers always helped with the introduction. In other words, they would try and encourage the class to understand the importance of the elderly man standing in front of them.

In every presentation, Herb witnessed a transformation. It happened when he started singing; their facial expressions would change. They tried to understand. They wanted to know about his adventures. They wanted to know about the time he was shot.

Herb felt the greatest sense of support when he spoke in front of other veterans. Whatever he talked about—fear, missing home, his wounds, his losses — they understood.

One evening, he started to organize all of the stories he told in the order that they occurred. He began to put together his very own book.

Lost in the sea of his old stories, Herb felt nostalgic. He dug out an old photo album and touched the photos of himself and Greta. When she was alive, they travelled twice to Australia, to Tahiti, Japan, and many other places. Herb thought about those times. He loved travelling with her. She made sure everything was organized and always planned their itinerary.

What will I do with myself? Herb thought.

He thought about Toastmasters. It was a distraction and he enjoyed the challenge, but he needed more. He wanted to escape—everything around him reminded him of Greta. It had been a year and a half since she passed.

Herb was emotional and determined.

"So I decided to drive from Truro to Alaska," he tells me. It was spring, 1994, and he was 73 years old, ready to escape.

Herb packed his mattress, sleeping bag, camp stove, and icebox into his van.

His neighbour Frank prodded him about his journey.

"You're not a kid anymore Herb," Frank said.

"Oh, I'm OK," Herb said, as he tried his best to organize his van. He wasn't going to let anybody stop him.

Herb felt he was doing the right thing when he saw Truro in his rear-view mirror. He gripped his steering wheel, determined to drive the great distance. He knew that driving away from Truro didn't mean driving away from his great loss. It was difficult living without Greta — eating alone, sleeping alone. He wanted to get away.

With every mile, tears streamed down his face.

He drove 4,000 miles to finally reach Fairbanks, Alaska.

"I must confess I was very lonesome at times. Especially when it was raining. I played some tapes but many were sad songs. My wife, Greta, had just passed away about a year and a half ago, and driving on a rainy day was hard on me. I must confess I cried many times," Herb wrote in his journal.

Herb drove the entire distance — 1,200 miles — of the Alaskan highway. The American army built the highway during the Second World War. The Canadian government supplied the materials.

Herb met a man during a stop for road construction. "Where abouts do you live?" Herb asked.

"322," the man replied, which meant nothing to Herb. He later learned that addresses along the Alaska Highway were identified by mileage.

The highway was constructed out of fears that the Japanese soldiers might invade Alaska and get a foothold on North America.

During his trip, Herb regretted not visiting Robert Service's log cabin, but it was hours away from Fairbanks. In the army, Herb carried one of his poetry books with him, "Rhymes of a Red Cross Man." Robert Service had served in the Canadian Army in the First World War.

He thought about the young woman he had met at Toastmasters who encouraged him to write a book about his experiences. He thought about some of the stories he wanted to include. That's when the name Cecil Woodard came to mind. Cecil was always granted a pass to leave camp and would go out on the town for the evening. He was always coming back drunk and the boys wanted to teach him a lesson. One night, Herb and two of his strong friends lifted each corner of Cecil Woodard's steel bed, careful not to wake him, and carried him to the middle of the parade square. Herb smiled at the thought of Cecil Woodard's face when the bugler woke him. It was shortly after that event that Herb transferred out of the Fourteenth Anti-Aircraft Battery.

He thought a lot about Cecil Woodard. He was one of the most memorable individuals Herb had ever met.

Herb decided that when he got home he would finish organizing his stories and write down as many memories of his experiences in training and war that he could remember. He wouldn't write about the terror, he would write about positive memories—memories that would become eternal through his writing.

He was proud of his trip to Alaska and proud that he accomplished another challenge. When Herb reached his home in Truro, he was only 200 miles short of driving 10,000 miles.

"I don't know how long it took because I stopped to see army buddies on my way there and back," Herb tells me, adding, "I was happy to be home."

He found a new sense of comfort, having travelled such a great distance on his own. He would be fine.

One day, as he flipped through the *Truro Daily News* and sipped on tea, he began to ponder. He had mastered bodybuilding, public speaking, and travelling as his hobbies...but what next? He popped a piece of bread in the toaster oven and stared at the little red light. He had just returned from Alaska and he was ready for something new.

He buttered his toast, got some cheese, and returned to the newspaper. He would brainstorm later.

With the turn of each page he smiled—he really enjoyed learning about what others in the community were doing.

Then, a headline in a tiny box in a right hand corner caught his eye.

"Parachute-training club in Stewiake," it read.

Shortly after Herb turned 74, he decided to parachute again. He thought it would be a great challenge.

Herb parachuting in Upper Stewiake.

His journey began in a small plane with a jumpmaster. Herb had one parachute strapped to his back and one strapped to his chest. He was given instructions of what to do in case his main chute didn't open, but he was nervous all the same.

His first thought was that if something went wrong while he was flying through the air, he'd be sure to pull the wrong handle.

The plane slowed to 100 miles an hour. Herb knew that he would be jumping soon. The jumpmaster gave the signal and he crawled on his hands and knees to the door. Herb slowly put his left foot out, trying to get it onto the little foot pedal. He had difficulty getting into position, and the wind blowing in his face did not help. Next, he had to grab the strut on the wing with his left hand. After sweating through the motions, and upon hearing the command, Herb jumped out of the plane. Those haunting words flooded his thoughts: *What the hell am I doing here?*

The jumpmaster told Herb that he was the oldest jumper he had ever had. "Well, I am glad I jumped," Herb said.

"Would you ever jump again?" The jumpmaster asked.

"No," Herb answered.

He was proud, though, that he jumped on his own and not in tandem.

On the drive home, the events of the day reminded Herb of a song, and he sang, "Oh, it's no, nay, never---no, nay, never no more, will I jump from an aircraft--no, never---no more!"

Once again, Herb returned to 17 Alice Street feeling proud. He had jumped out of a plane! He didn't think he could possibly top that challenge.

The next day Herb felt exhilarated from his accomplishment. Instead of opening the paper that morning he took a large lined pad of paper and began making a list of places he'd dreamt of visiting—Vimy Ridge, back to Rome, the Mediterranean, China, Egypt—then put his pen down. He didn't have to write a list to know that he wanted to travel the world.

Herb knew he had to see it all. But his daydreaming was interrupted by the telephone in his study. He made his way into his little office.

"Hello, Herb here," he said.

He was never the best at talking on the phone.

"You don't say..." he said. His eyes shone and he let out a booming laugh.

Nimbus Publishing was calling and his book of short stories, 'The LightHearted Soldier', would be published in January.

"Thank you, so much." he said, hanging up the phone.

He threw his hands in the air and closed his eyes.

All of his memories—of his best friends, of their pranks and most importantly, meeting Greta, would be documented forever.

He spent the spring travelling around Nova Scotia, promoting his book and giving talks.

One morning, he brought the *Truro Daily News* and his tea outside to the little table outside his back door. He wiped the water from the seat and set his things down.

He looked around his backyard and remembered the way his father had cared for his garden. Herb didn't know a thing about gardening or flowers. He knew that one type of flower was perennial while the other was annual—but he didn't know where to begin.

He decided it was time to learn. He joined a group at the Nova Scotia Agricultural College where he could learn the proper ways of planting and harvesting.

"That's where I met Karen," he tells me, grinning.

On his first day he felt nervous. Everyone seemed to be a lot younger than him, and they looked like they knew what they were doing.

"Do you want some help?" asked a woman who was one row over from Herb.

"Yes—I may not be using the right tool," he said. "I'm Herb Peppard."

"Nice to meet you Herb, I'm Karen Taylor," she said.

Herb thought that Karen was an attractive and kind 33-year-old woman.

He didn't have intentions of dating Karen because he didn't think that a 33-year-old would have any interest in him.

One day, he said hi to her at the Superstore where she was working at the time and, "that was it," he says, smiling. The next time he saw her in gardening class, he invited her over for soup and she accepted. He continued inviting her over for supper, and that's how they became acquainted.

Soon, they were spending every weekend together.

One evening before Karen came for dinner, Herb was organizing his notebooks and disposing of old newspapers that had piled in the kitchen when he came across his old travel list. He had spent so many weekends with Karen that he had forgotten about his list.

#1. Vimy Ridge

He stared at his writing. He had written this note quite a while ago—but Herb saves everything.

Herb decided it was time to start crossing things off his list. Every New Year's Day, from then on, he sat down and wrote his annual list of goals for the year and each list included a big trip. He reached his travelling goals almost every year.

In 2000, Herb visited Vimy Ridge because of its historical significance as a turning point of the First World War. Herb was fascinated by the names of 11,285 Canadians engraved on the monument that stands at Vimy Ridge. Many of the gravestones did not have names. Instead, they were carved with, "A Canadian Soldier, known unto God." This wasn't the first time Herb was there, however, this visit made a big impression on him. In 2003 he represented his legion and attended celebrations at Juno Beach in France.

The very next year, Herb met the president of the United States, George W. Bush, at the American embassy in Rome. As a veteran of the First Special Service Force, Herb was invited to hear the president speak. Herb and his fellow veterans were guests of honour and the American president spoke to them. The FSSF received this honour because they were the first Allied army unit to enter Rome on the day it was liberated. The event in Rome marked the 60th anniversary of a liberated Rome. Herb was alongside 14 veterans; eight Canadians, six Americans, and their family members. It was a momentous occasion and the president spoke highly of Herb's unit. Herb thought about that particular day when he was in the Naples hospital after being shot in the leg. He was grateful he got to celebrate on this day and in Rome.

During Herb's visit to Rome, he and his group spent time at the American embassy and the Canadian ambassador's villa. He also visited the Italian president, Carlo Azeglio Ciampi, at his home. Herb was honoured to be able to see Pope John Paul II speak to a crowd of hundreds at St. Peter's Square at the Vatican. Herb was enthralled with the beauty of Rome, and questioned how he would ever return to Truro, where the meals were incomparable.

While Herb was in Italy, he and his group visited the Commonwealth Cemetery, which was close to Anzio.

Thousands of headstones represent soldiers from Canada, England, Scotland, India, and other Commonwealth countries. The cemetery was immaculate, Herb felt as though he was standing on a plush green carpet. It was full of flowers.

Herb walked around the cemetery until he found a stone that read, "First Special Service Force." There was an entire section devoted to Herb's unit. Immediately Herb found six of his friends, and found himself standing in front of the graves of two buddies who had been inseparable during the war. Their names and ages were engraved: Private R.G. Briddon, 21, and Sgt. J. MacIver, 20. He remembered these two men as always being together. They were always singing and joking around. Herb felt tears well in his eyes, and he knew that if he tried to speak, he would cry.

It seemed like yesterday that Briddon and MacIver had their arms around each other, kicking up their legs, combat boots on and singing.

Despite the quiet of the cemetery, Herb could still hear the voices of his friends singing.

"There were many thoughts pouring through my mind that afternoon," he tells me, thinking back.

He left the cemetery that day with great feelings of loss and exhilaration. He had seen two of his closest friends lying side by side and for a moment, they weren't even separated by death. It was as if they were with him again.

Herb continued his list by travelling to the Mediterranean—on a cruise with Karen and his brother Bill, sister-in-law Betty, son and daughter-in-law Herb Jr. and Deborah. Another year he travelled with two of his brothers, Albert and Bill, to Egypt. The following couple of years Herb made solo trips, one to China and one to India.

ten

"I wasn't a perfect soldier."

Herb Peppard

"This is my grandson, Mosher," Herb says as he and Mosher, Rosalee's son, make their way into my parents' home in Truro one evening in late December.

Mosher is named after Greta's brother who had been in the First Canadian Parachute Battalion. Greta's brother was killed just before the end of the war. He fought in the battle of Normandy and was relaxing in the grass, the end of war so near, when he was shot by a lone sniper.

"That's who I was named after," Mosher says proudly.

"I got word of some exciting news," Herb says, his eyes twinkling. He and Mosher take a seat in the living room. Herb sips on water while Mosher polishes off a Tim Hortons coffee.

"My unit is going to be awarded the Congressional Gold Medal of Honour in February in Washington," he says, adding that he plans to attend the ceremony.

"I can't wait," he says.

This will be the highest honour Herb has been awarded for his participation in World War Two, although he has received high praise and recognition in Canada.

"In 2008, I received the most exciting letter in the mail, I must have told you about this one," he says.

The letter came from the army base in Petawawa, Ontario. Herb was invited to the regimental dinner to present the Sergeant Herbert Peppard Silver Star trophy for the first time to a selected Canadian Special Operations Regiment (CSOR) Top Operator.

"I remember thinking then that I couldn't believe that I was given this tremendous honour," he tells me.

He climbed mountains, rowed rubber boats and marched for miles. He parachuted from airplanes. He obeyed all orders and attended parades. There was just one imperfection among his successes as a soldier; his AWOLs.

"I suppose that they had looked past my history and focused on the positive aspects of my career as a soldier," he says.

The "S/SGT. G. H. PEPPARD Award" is "presented to a NCM of the regiment whose actions and conduct best exemplifies the spirit of a special operations non-commissioned member. The trophy is named after S/SGT G.H Peppard, SS, BSM, who as a Canadian member of the FSSF performed in an exemplary fashion during combat and earned the Silver Star."

Herb's award is presented each year, recognizing the abilities of the named recipient who achieved the high standard set by Herb and his fellow comrades.

"Depending on the circumstance, I try my best to travel to Petawawa, Ontario, to present the award that bears my name," he says.

"But, oh boy, Washington would be exciting."

Moving into the dining room, and taking a seat at the table, Herb and his grandson burst into song.

"We wish you a Merry Christmas, we wish you a Merry Christmas!" Herb and Mosher belt from the bottom of their hearts as they await my mother's meal.

"We're singing for our supper!" Mosher yells, sharing the same enthusiasm as his granddad.

Herb entertains the table with stories about his family. "My sister Louise also lives in Truro, she's two years older than me—96," he says, adding that she lives alone.

"We talk every night on the phone after *Jeopardy!*"

Following dinner, we make our way back into the living room. Herb asks if we would be interested in hearing him recite a poem.

"I've always loved poetry and I would like to recite a poem by my favourite poet, Robert Service," he says. Relaxing by the crackling fire, seated comfortably in a wingback chair, Herb's blue eyes glisten as he takes a deep breath.

"I may not remember all of the words," he says with a smile. But then, he puts on a theatrical performance and recites the 110-line poem, "Fleurette," by heart.

epilogue

Herb and his children in Italy

"This is from our trip to Italy," Herb says sliding a big photograph of himself and his three children at the very site of one of the battles he fought in alongside his unit.

Herb was proud to have his children with him in Italy. He describes the mountains as being blanketed in poppies.

This was the fourth time Herb had been to Italy. Of course the first was 68 years before, a much different experience than this peaceful, yet emotional adventure. He was pleased to take his three adult children to the mountains, beaches, villages, towns, and cities that he helped liberate nearly 70 years earlier.

"Yes, we had a great time," he says.

Then, he tells me a story about his first tour of Italy.

He saw a man come out of a house and walk along his garden.

All of a sudden there was an explosion—either a landmine or artillery.

The man was gone. A woman and two small children ran out from their farmhouse. Herb watched as they stumbled over the uneven ground to where the explosion happened.

It was December 4, 1943, only a day after their baptism of fire, when he watched a family torn apart.

"Our Italian tour guide, Gianni Blasi, knew a lot about the First Special Service Force and studied where we served and fought," Herb says.

"So I told him about the farmhouse and the man who lost his life that day in his garden," he adds.

Gianni knew where the force's basecamp at Monte La Difensa was, and he said that the farmhouse is still standing in the field nearby.

Gianni took Herb and his family in his car and they drove toward the house. They stopped about 50 yards away. Herb recognized the house right away. It looked the same.

"It was an emotional day for me," he says.

He tells me it was shortly after his 92nd birthday, and before his trip with his children to Italy, that Karen took a job in Washington, D.C. They had been companions for 16 years—"my lady friend," he calls her.

They still talk on the phone every day.

Herb had a major setback in September 2012, when he fell in his home. The fall resulted in a hairline fracture in his right hip and he spent six months in the Camp Hill Veteran's Memorial building, which is part of the Halifax Infirmary. One of Herb's doctors said that few patients—especially Herb's age — recover after taking a fall like his. But Herb wouldn't have it any other way. After a lot of rest and physiotherapy, he was able to walk again. He started off slowly but now he walks a mile every day.

Herb's three children—Herb (the fourth), Lark, and Rosalee are all married with children. Herb Jr. lives in Australia with his wife, Deborah and he has two children, Isabel and Herbert the fifth from his previous marriage. Herb Jr., is retired and spends time with his family.

Herb's daughter Lark, lives in Ottawa with her husband Carmen, and they have three married children; Candle and her husband John Larkin, Oak and his wife Cathy, and Ginger and her husband Brian Lafave. Lark also has three grandchildren; Candle and John have two girls, Sky and Summer; and Oak and Cindy have a son, Ashton.

Rosalee lives in Oshawa with her husband Allan and they have two sons, Luke and Mosher.

Four of Herb's siblings are still living; his older sister Louise Fielding lives in Truro, Nova Scotia. Of his younger siblings, his brother Albert lives in Middleton, Nova Scotia with his wife Kaye; his sister Betty Cummings lives in Charlottetown, Prince Edward Island; and his brother Bill lives with his wife Betty in Moncton, New Brunswick.

Recently, Herb lost his eldest sibling, Dorothy 'Dot.' She was 101 and spent most of her life in Montreal. Herb's siblings Iola, Patricia, and Raymond have also passed away.

Herb is still good friends with George Tratt and George Wright—both original members of the First Special Service Force. A black and white photograph of George Smith (Smitty) remains on his fridge. Herb wrote in one of his short stories that he grieved his friend's death for a long time, and he may not ever fully get over the loss of his best friend.

Currently, Herb is living in the very house where he was born and raised on Alice Street in Truro, Nova Scotia. He writes stories about family and war, which are published in his column, 'Dispatches,' in the local newspaper, the *Truro Daily News*.

Herb, alongside members of the First Special Service Force, was awarded the Congressional Gold Medal in the Capitol building in Washington D.C. on February 3, 2015. The night before the ceremony, 42 members of the force – 14 Canadians and 28 Americans – their families and friends, gathered at the Sheraton hotel. In an emotional introduction, each member rose and waved when their name was called by the Master of Ceremonies.

More than 70 years before, the First Special Service Force stormed Anzio Beachhead—and the surviving members were finally recognized with Congress' highest honour.

In a passionate speech, House Speaker John Boehner introduced the First Special Service Force.

"For every man they lost—they killed 25. For every man captured – they took 235. The force was so fierce, the enemy dubbed them the 'Devil's.' So effective, today our special forces refer to them as pioneers. Today we bestow on them our highest honour," said Boehner.

"I couldn't sleep the night before, I was too excited," Herb told me after the ceremony. "The speeches were emotional – they brought tears to my eyes."

Herb and his daughters. Lark (left) and Rosalee following the Congressional Gold Medal ceremony in Washington D.C.

Gonna Live Forever by Herb Peppard

I'm gonna live forever
got a master plan
if my dreams come true I'll be
The Eternal Man
I'll visit all the health stores
eat yogurt by the pail
and exercise my body
till I'm hard as nails

I'm gonna live forever
that's a real safe bet
I'm gonna live forever
that's a goal I've set
I'm gonna live forever
there's no use denyin'
I'm gonna live forever
or I'll die tryin'!!!

I've given up tobacco
and I don't eat sweets
thrown out eggs and butter

I avoid all meats
I jog seven miles a day
in the sun or rain
I'm gonna live forever
I don't mind the pain!

I take all the vitamins
from "A" up to "Z"
I'll even miss my breakfast
take a pill instead
I've thrown out tea and coffee
never take a sup
I'm gonna live forever
I just won't give up

list of recognition

Military Distinctions Canada:

    Italy Star

    France and Germany Star

    Defence Medal

    Canadian Volunteer Service Medal with Silver Bar

    War Medal 1939-1945

Military Distinctions USA:

    Congressional Gold Medal

    USA Silver Star (awarded for gallantry in action)

USA Bronze Star (awarded for heroism/outstanding achievement)

USA Army Combat Infantry Badge

USA Army airborne Wings Badge

Awards and Recognition

1980: Bachelor of Education, Dalhousie University, Halifax

1981: Atlantic Bodybuilding Championship Award for years of Loyalty and Support to the sport of Bodybuilding

1983: (age 63) Nova Scotia Masters Bodybuilding Champion (40 and older)

1984: P.E.I.A.B.B.A Award for Inspiration and Dedication to the sport of Bodybuilding

1986: N.S. A.B.B.A Award for Outstanding Service to the sport of bodybuilding

1988: (age 68) Nova Scotia Masters Bodybuilding Champion (2nd win)

1993: YMCA Canada Peace Medal

1994: Nova Scotia Toastmasters Champion (twice)

2002:Life Membership Award, Royal Canadian Legion: Branch 26, Truro

2002: Queen's Golden Jubilee Medal

2008: Canadian Military CSOR Inaugural Annual "Sergeant Herbert Peppard Silver Star Award"

2010: Sports Heritage Society: MacQuarrie's Pharmasave Outstanding Male Senior Athlete Award

2012: Queens Diamond Jubilee Medal

2012: Honorary Century of Service Award

acknowledgement

Thank you Herb Peppard—for sharing your memories with me, some dating back 70 years. You taught me that determination, love, and optimism will help overcome life's most difficult challenges. It's been an absolute pleasure.

I'd like to thank Herb's daughter, Lark Hewer. Lark helped me sift through dates, facts, and specific details about her dad's life. I couldn't have done this without you.

To my family, thank you for your help, encouragement, and for sharing my excitement.

I want to thank Joanna Iossifidis for her graphic work. Joanna designed the front and back of the book, the map, and she edited all of the photographs. Joanna worked tirelessly on the graphics for Herbert Peppard: The Eternal Man.

I'd like to thank Angele Boudreau, for taking Herb's photograph for the book, and for helping with additional edits. Thank you Chantal, Kaitlyn, Kelsey and Amanda for your edits, suggestions and generosity.

Thanks to all of my friends and family who have helped along the way. Writing Herb Peppard's biography has been an honour and a privilege.

about the author

Janice Dickson is an Ottawa-based political reporter with iPolitics. She began covering Parliament Hill shortly after graduating from Western University's Master of Arts in journalism program in June 2014. Janice also holds a Bachelor of Arts in theatre and English from Acadia University. Originally from Truro, Nova Scotia, Janice met Herb in June 2012 and they've been friends ever since.